UNSTOPPABLE

Your guide to wealth, prosperity and financial freedom

Mensah Oteh

Also by Mensah Oteh

The Best Chance

The Good Life

Wisdom Keys in words

Unlocking Life's Treasure Chest

First Print, 2017 ISBN: 978-1545311004

ACKNOWLEDGEMENTS

To my mentors: your words of wisdom changed my life and I am forever indebted to you.

To my friends who offered encouragement, support, and prayers — I am grateful.

To my family, thank you. I love you.

CONTENTS

PART 5
MAKING THE MOST IMPORTANT DECISION

PART 6
PLAYING THE GAME TO WIN

INTRODUCTION

At the age of thirty the average person has worked for at least ten years, which is usually sufficient time to have discovered their purpose, discerned some of their gifts, abilities, talents and skills, and put to work a good plan towards their future. Therefore, if you live and were raised in a free country, and aren't financially free by the age of thirty, don't blame the government or the state of the economy. It isn't due to your company or your boss. Bad luck, fate, or destiny aren't to blame. It's all down to you because you don't have a good plan. You lack discipline, you haven't conditioned yourself for wealth, and you have self-limiting beliefs about wealth and don't have a compelling reason to be financially free.

If reading the above makes you feel uneasy or even angry, your reaction might inspire you to change your thoughts, beliefs and actions so you become all you can be – and financially free in the process.

The word 'wealth' is understood differently by different people. It brings to our hearts and minds a variety of emotions, images and memories, some of which may be in conflict. For some people wealth is simply having the financial means to fulfil their life's purpose or satisfy their desires. To others it means financial freedom and a state of being debt free. It can mean having a multimillionaire or billionaire status and lifestyle, or abundance and the experience of all that life has freely given us.

The way you define wealth not only determines whether you're wealthy or not but also (and more importantly) whether you become or remain wealthy. True wealth should be mental, emotion, spiritual, physical and material, and it should be evident in the areas that you need to experience to live the good life such as happiness, joy, love, good health, success, prosperity, spirituality, abundance, fulfilment, wisdom, purpose, growth, significance, productivity, and living effectively.

Your experience of true wealth can be manifested on three levels: the spiritual, the mental or psychological, and the material level. The spiritual level is the highest and brings with it the realisation that you are wealth, and wealth is not external or separate to who you are. All the wealth you need is within you and simply needs to be expressed. The mental or psychological level is where you recognise that wealth is a product of your mind based on your thoughts – what you think, you become and create. The third and lowest level is the physical manifestation of wealth in material form, and this is where your material possessions are evident as a reward for your actions. To experience true wealth you need to experience all three levels.

In this book I focus on the third and final level of wealth – the material level – which produces financial freedom. I will show you simple strategies you can use to achieve financial freedom by converting your time, energy, intellect and effort into money. Why is this important? Well, your goal should be financial freedom because it offers you the freedom to live the extraordinary life –life on your terms, one filled with passion, abundance, fulfilment, excitement, joy, freedom and peace. Although being in a strong financial position isn't a pre-requisite for wealth, it can provide a platform or environment to support a wealthy state of mind if the intent and purpose supporting your desire is right.

Whenever we talk about money or financial wealth, we tend to measure ourselves against someone who has less or more than us. Financial wealth is relative, and achieving financial freedom is your duty, responsibility and obligation. You have the potential to be financially free – you have the potential, abilities and power within to help you be who you wish to be, do what you want to and have anything you desire. But that potential is activated by choice. You are engineered for success and have greatness in you but to experience it you must make the right choices and take the right action.

Financial freedom is created from inspiration, not intellect. If you can find your inspiration and remain inspired, you can be wealthy. The fact that you're reading this book is proof that you desire a significant and meaningful life. If you're willing to apply the principles outlined here, you can achieve financial freedom and wealth. The outlined principles and strategies are infallible when applied diligently and correctly.

Why I wrote this book

Financially free at thirty, I retired from my engineering profession three years later, allowing me to reclaim the remaining years of my life. My current freedom has given me the opportunity to discover and follow my true life's purpose and passion.

I'm not from a family of means – quite the opposite. And I didn't fall on good fortune. I arrived in London as a poor African student and yet became financially free within eight years despite having debts and not earning a high income.

My story shows how the financial wealth and freedom model that has been taught for so many years isn't only wrong and obsolete, it has also kept many from living the abundant life they deserve. You don't need millions in your bank account or to have multiple assets. You don't need to have a six figure income, and you don't need to win the lottery to become financially free.

You simply need a plan and to work that plan.

How will this book make you wealthy?

If you dedicate yourself to applying the strategies in this book, you will achieve financial freedom, and if you make this book part of your life, it will make you wealthy beyond your dreams.

The ideas in the book form the foundation of my life, but more importantly they're the same wealth strategies used by the successful and wealthy. By using them you'll be able to:

- Get yourself started on the journey to financial freedom
- Get out of debt in the shortest possible time whilst continuing to build your net worth

- Internalise and adopt the wealth philosophies, habits and lifestyles of the wealthy without losing your unique personality
- Use leverage to achieve your dreams more quickly
- Prepare your financial and wealth statement to gain clarity about your financial position
- Prepare a wealth plan with specific strategies so you can reach your goals
- Select the right investment vehicle and plan unique to you
- Rid yourself of any negative conditioning you might have about money
- Create, protect, multiply and share your wealth

This isn't a book filled with empty promises; it offers hope, inspiration, motivation, education and change. It will stretch your thinking, challenge some of your beliefs, and encourage you to ask yourself empowering questions – a necessary pre-requisite to building wealth. People who are financially free and wealthy aren't better, smarter or more gifted than you. They simply think differently, act differently and live differently to the rest of the population – and so can you.

Put the advice in this book to work and rewrite your future. *You can't lose with the stuff I use.*

Part 1

STARTING THE JOURNEY

CHAPTER 1

GROUND ZERO: YOU ARE WEALTHY

The greatest wealth is a poverty of desires.
— *Lucius Annaeus Seneca*

If I told you that you are among the wealthiest people in the world today, would you agree? If you did, what would you consider your real assets to be? If not, what's missing in your life? I don't mean tangible assets or material possessions alone. Wealth is much more, and you possess incalculable wealth, if not in money, then in ideas, opportunities, knowledge, abilities, potential, skills and talents. Your philosophy, beliefs, and attitude towards wealth decide whether or not you experience *true* wealth.

Most of what you have or need to experience the abundant life is free; the air you breathe, the love in you, your loved ones and friends, your ability to laugh, a good night's rest, and your happy memories. To begin your wealth journey you must start with an attitude of gratitude because this changes your focus from one of expectation and accumulation to one of appreciation and celebration. Appreciating what you have unlocks the gate to all three levels of wealth.

Gratitude begins with recognising who you are and what life has freely given you. Most people don't feel wealthy because they're trying

3

to pursue something external that they believe they need to feel complete on the inside. Material wealth *is* important but it should succeed, not precede, true wealth.

True wealth is a product of your mind based on your focus. If you focus on how you can obtain more material possessions to the exclusion of the first two levels, you won't be wealthy. And the spiritual and mental levels of wealth won't produce material wealth until the principles of wealth creation, multiplication, and protection have been mastered and applied consistently.

How was I able to achieve financial freedom within eight years? Am I gifted or exceptionally talented? Did I come from an affluent family? Was it luck, destiny, or did I fall on good fortune? None of these.

I come from humble beginnings. Although I was raised by a remarkable father and an amazing mother, we were financially challenged. There were periods in my early childhood when having two meals a day was a cause for celebration. But we were wealthy at heart because we lived from a place of abundance, love, hope, joy and gratitude. This laid the foundation for building my dream of financial freedom – I knew I was wealthy within so it was easier to express and manifest it without.

My starting point was a refusal to remain imprisoned by the environment in which I was born. I decided that the circumstances under which I was raised would not be part of my future and would certainly not hold me back. A burning desire for a better life for me and for my family, combined with a passion to do something significant, led me to emigrate from my native Nigeria to the UK in pursuit of a new and better life.

I arrived in London with only a dream. Although I had no friends or family, and also no money, I knew in my heart that the picture of the future I had created in my imagination would become reality if I gave it a chance. When I first arrived I ran into severe financial challenges, some tough enough to break anyone's spirit, but in the midst of this I found grace and the strength to persevere. And I soon discovered that my desire and passion had to be combined with principles and strategies for success.

4

To begin with, I studied the financial practices of a few remarkably wealthy people; I listened, learned and paid close attention to every word I heard from my mentors. If I could replicate their thinking patterns, habits and behaviour, I reasoned I could discover my own path to freedom and wealth. But I also learned from their mistakes, setbacks, challenges and failures. To be wealthy, you have to study wealth. To be successful, you have to study success.

Next I decided it was time to replicate their success by modelling their beliefs, philosophies, decisions and actions. Eventually, my thinking, attitudes and vocabulary changed. And at this point I knew my future was ready for me.

Success leaves behind clues. The best thing you can do for yourself if you wish to see your dreams become reality is to find success and replicate it.

There are two ways of learning – through your mistakes or through mentors. You won't reach your highest potential if you learn through your personal experience and mistakes alone. Every great person stood proudly on the shoulders of another, and you should have no shame in doing the same. By combining your experiences with the wisdom gained through other people's experiences you can propel yourself ten or fifteen years ahead.

All our decisions are driven by the need to gain pleasure or avoid pain. My personal breakthrough was when I realised that the pain of remaining where I was, and accepting the card life had dealt me, was much greater than the sacrifice I had to make to get to where I wanted to be. Until success becomes a must, you will compromise on your dreams. When you truly resolve that you won't accept a life below your true potential, your life will change.

Most people believe that to create financial wealth you need to have money, but nothing could be further from the truth. All you need is to make a choice. You simply need to give yourself permission – to dream, decide and take action. It really is that simple.

If I can do it, so can you. I am no different to you. You have what it takes to make your dreams reality, and no one is smarter or better than you. You have:

- A mind and imagination to help you create any future you want
- Your memory to guide you from repeating any previous errors in judgement
- A heart for discerning, making decisions and to support your intuition
- Your body, a support system unique to you alone to give you energy for your journey
- Willpower to give you the strength and resolve to never give up
- A conscience to serve as an internal referee to guide your every step along the way
- The power of choice to help you choose your destiny
- All the wisdom of the world available within your reach to provide good counsel
- Life stories of other successful people that you can learn from and replicate
- Unlimited potential, with gifts, talents and skills to support you

You have it all; you simply need to take a chance.

CHAPTER 2

IT'S ON YOU: ACCOUNTABILITY

No man ever steps in the same river twice, for it's not the same river and he's not the same man.

— *Heraclitus of Ephesus*

Life expects that everything created or made should become all it can be and reach its highest potential. With all life has freely given you, comes the responsibility to become the best you can be in all areas – health, success, prosperity, happiness, joy, spirituality, growth, productivity and financial wealth.

Financial wealth is a product of who you are (your character), not only what you have. Financial wealth (money and your assets) is an extension of your personality because you give part of you for it. It takes all of you to earn money – your time, intellect, energy, imagination, and presence. You exchange a piece of your life for it because it's an essential part of living.

We spend approximately forty hours each week working for money, but few of us take the time to study the one thing we exchange more than half our lives for. Those who become wealthy are those who study money. To succeed in any area of life you should begin by finding out how things work; financial freedom is a study, a design, a practice, and finally a lifestyle. Most people aren't financially free because they have never made it a must, or they've made the common mistake of delegating responsibility for their financial future to someone else. *You* are responsible for your own financial success or failure.

To begin your journey to financial freedom you have to accept complete responsibility for your life. This goes beyond words and feelings; it should be evident in your actions. You play a part in the outcomes of your life. Although you can't control all events or circumstances, you can choose how you react or respond. Our decisions create our experiences and there are no victims in life – *we are all volunteers.*

For many years I held onto a victim mindset and this limited me. I felt life was unfair and I could come up with a million reasons why things hadn't worked out and why it wasn't my fault. But my life changed when I accepted I was a volunteer in my life and nothing happened without my participation and consent. This was difficult to accept initially, but as I exposed myself to more wisdom, I couldn't find a single piece of evidence that supported my previously flawed philosophy. For things to change in my life, I had to change.

A lack of responsibility combined with a rejection of wisdom leads to poverty and shame. Irrespective of where you were born or the circumstances under which you were raised, life will present you with the opportunity for a better future, but first you must give up complaining and blaming and accept that you are the problem. This will empower you to also see yourself as the solution, and then you will be able to take the necessary steps to bring about the changes you need.

Most people wait for the economy to get better, for government leaders to change, for external circumstances to change, or for good fortune to befall them. But history shows that things seldom change. People, on the other hand, do. You are the only variable in the equation that you have direct control over, and you can change your circumstances quickly by working on yourself.

To create your financial future, you must begin within.

CHAPTER 3

WHAT COMES FIRST: REASONS, PASSION AND PRIORITIES

You cannot parcel out freedom in pieces because freedom is all or nothing.
— *Quintus Septimius Florens Tertullianus*

When I ask people to name the single greatest value of life (outside life itself), to my delight many give the same answer – *freedom*.

So why don't we pursue freedom? Why isn't it a definite purpose and goal for all of us? In most countries, people live in occupational and economic slavery – their lifestyles, working hours, working conditions, vacations, employment terms, and even some family related matters are influenced (and in many cases controlled) by others.

They are free in the natural sense, but few truly live like they are free, and fewer still live the abundant life. Daily they invest their time, energy, effort, focus, knowledge, wisdom, and presence towards fulfilling other people's dreams and goals rather than their own. They focus on earning a living instead of designing a life, and they follow other people's plans because they have none of their own. Freedom eludes them.

To become financially independent, freedom (and the pursuit of the other benefits that come with being wealthy) must become your obsession, an absolute must for you, something you're unwilling to live without. Until you decide you aren't willing to live without freedom, you will compromise your standards and settle for security instead of abundance.

To make a change you have to make a decision for yourself, for your family, and for the people whose lives could be made better through your support. That starts by choosing to work for your goals and dreams and not for your boss, a pay cheque or a company.

Why not give your dream a chance? Working for your dreams and goals will not only bring you fulfilment, it will also reward you with the highest level of achievement.

You should also set a goal to be financially free, because like any goal it helps you move in the direction of your potential. It isn't what you get, it is who you become that's most important. Achieving your goal should be of secondary importance, and your focus should be on becoming the kind of person who *deserves* your goal.

Imagine you're eighty-five and on a rocking chair. As you sit there rocking, you replay your life's journey. What aspects would you wish were different? What would you wish you'd experienced or changed? You don't have to wait until the end of your life to discover things that make you unhappy. Change the script now. Choose your destiny now!

You can change your life, you can be free, and you can live a life free from regret. All you need is a reason to get started.

Desire

Everything begins as a thought or an idea, and you can develop the smallest and most insignificant idea into a Mount Everest of concepts through a burning desire. Wealth creation is no different. It has to become a strong desire in you or you won't pursue it.

Financial wealth is attracted to you based on the level of importance you associate with having it. Money has ears and eyes and it is attracted to you based on what you say about it, how much desire you have for it, and (importantly) what you do with that desire. If you haven't set financial freedom as a goal, it will elude you. You can only become wealthy by choice, and making that choice starts with making money a necessity and a priority.

To become financially free you need a burning desire combined with passion. A desire is something you want but passion is something you're unwilling to live without. When you develop a sincere burning desire, the potential and passion within you will serve as fuel to get you off the launch pad to your dreams and goals.

Reasons

First, you need to understand why you want to be financially free. Your reasons must be strong and compelling in order for you to remain on your journey and reach your destination. Your reasons will pull you forward and through the difficult times, the obstacles and the challenges you face. Find your why. Be specific, because if you can combine your reasons with desire, passion and persistence, and the willingness to work, you will become wealthy.

Before reading further, stop for a few minutes. Pick up your journal and crystallise your thinking by writing down a list of reasons why you want to be financially free. Recruit your heart, body and mind as you make your list. Think of everything you can, big or small. For example, some of my reasons include:

- Abundance: to have the means to meet my needs, wants and desires
- Security: to create a secure and safe future for myself, my family and loved ones
- Freedom: so I can work for joy and not out of necessity
- Purpose: to fulfil my life's purpose and calling
- Fun: to live life to the fullest
- Lifestyle: to experience a lifestyle of luxury
- Legacy: to leave a good legacy
- Significance: to make a difference and create good experiences for others
- Benevolence: to give away as much as I can
- Peace of mind

11

- Passion: to do what I love
- Responsibility: to maximise my potential and allow the greatness in me to be exposed
- Significance: to make a difference and create good experiences for others

This is your list, so don't worry about what other people might think. You will be paying the price for everything on your list and you owe no one an explanation.

With your reasons documented, you must become clear about your values. Take the time you need to review (and question) your rules. Question your beliefs before you begin. You should be open minded because your beliefs and rules will change, especially if you are willing to grow. That's fine, but it's important to keep your values intact because they will serve as your guiding compass.

Priorities

Once you've documented your reasons and values, it's time to identify your priorities and rank them in order of importance. Wealth and money shouldn't replace more important areas in your life, so establish your priorities before beginning your journey. Success without fulfilment will lead to regret. Often, we lack fulfilment because we lose sight of our values and are drawn towards non-priorities. Priorities protect you from making unwise decisions and also guide you in the direction you wish to travel, ensuring you get to your intended destination.

We allocate our time, effort and energy according to our priorities but without clearly defined priorities, we are often distracted by secondary activities. My personal priorities (in order of importance) are:

- God: his will and purpose for my life
- My family and loved ones
- My health and well being
- Business and finances

Many people say that their family is the most important priority. However, few spend more than an hour of quality time with their family every day. This isn't because they don't want to; it's because their priorities aren't clear.

All priorities are not equal, and the order and importance assigned to each determines its value. Financial freedom is important, and the order and the importance you assign to money will make a difference to whether your journey is memorable and exciting or not.

Although money is important to me, it is at the bottom of my list of priorities. However, it can help me enjoy my top four priorities, and because it's a facilitator, I take it seriously.

By managing your priorities you teach yourself not to sacrifice what matters most for something of lesser importance. Always keep the main thing, the main thing. If you identify and protect your priorities, they will eventually become your habits and part of your lifestyle.

Part 2

LAY DEEP FOUNDATIONS
BEFORE YOU BEGIN

CHAPTER 4

FIRST STEP: KNOW THE TRUTH

To accomplish great things, we must not only act, but also dream; not only plan, but also believe.

— Anatole France

Financial freedom is having sufficient personal wealth to live the remainder of your life without needing to rely on outside financial support or having to work unless you choose to.

It has little to do with private jets, supercars, yachts, mansions, and luxury lifestyles. The movies, the media and a few people's lifestyles have diluted the true essence of what freedom means. It isn't about accumulation alone, rather it means arriving at a place where nothing (especially your possessions) has complete ownership and control over your life or your family.

What does financial freedom mean to you? How would you define it and what will your typical day look like if money weren't a necessity and you had the resources to meet your financial needs? Can you describe in detail what your average day would include?

- Where and what time would you wake up?
- What would you have for breakfast?
- What would you do once you are awake?
- How would you spend your day?
- Who would you spend it with?

Most people who are financially free are fulfilled and live the life they want, working harder and longer than they did when it was a necessity. This is because they are working from a place of a freedom and fulfilment rather than one of security and scarcity. If your dream is to become wealthy so you don't have to work another day in your life, you have it wrong and probably don't have what it takes to become and remain financially free.

Financial wealth begins by changing the way you think, which involves ridding yourself of old beliefs and making room for newer more empowering beliefs and philosophies congruent with wealth. If you aren't financially free today, it's likely that some of your beliefs need to be replaced. And so you must begin by identifying the beliefs that don't serve you and are stopping you from experiencing the life you deserve. Start by clearing out the garbage in the room of your mind to create space for new furniture to be brought in.

Debunking the myths

There are several myths about wealth and financial freedom, but the truth will set you free.

Myth 1: Many people adhere to the wrong definition of what it means to be financially wealthy, independent or free. And we often over-estimate the amount needed to achieve financial freedom. In our heads we have a picture of a financial statement with a lots of assets and a bank account with many zeros and a few commas. But the actual amount required to be financially free is much less. Whilst it's important to know what your financial dream number is, remember that your lifestyle will change according to your needs and desires. Financial freedom isn't about how much money you have in the bank or how many assets you own. Financial freedom is hidden in the four letter word 'free', meaning you are free from the fear, stress and worries of money matters. There are lots of people with hundreds of thousands, or even millions, in the bank who live in fear and from a place of scarcity and aren't truly free. They're afraid of losing everything in a market crash and live in fear. Others are terrified they will outlive their money so they operate from a place of lack, and this drives them to make money a master and themselves a slave. Some also have a lifestyle that keeps them hostage to money.

Freedom begins in your thoughts and is evident in your lifestyle.

Myth 2: Most people believe that financial wealth is measured in monetary terms (your net worth) alone; this assumption isn't wrong, but it's incomplete. Wealth is measured in money as a function of *time* and not of money alone. If you understand this, you're in a great position to achieve personal financial wealth. Your journey to financial freedom begins with understanding investment income flow, not earned income or net worth. To be financially free you need continuous income created from investment assets that are capable of generating money continuously and independently of your time investment. The income you generate must be greater than your expenses and must leave you with an income/expense ratio greater than 1. If you have this, you are wealthy (in time). The higher the ratio, the greater your wealth.

It's really that simple.

Instead of focusing on trying to increase your net worth by accumulating a fixed amount of money or assets with a fixed value, focus on acquiring assets that produce positive income whilst increasing in value. To become wealthy you need assets that produce a daily, monthly or yearly income greater than your expenses. More importantly, these assets should be capable of generating income without you having to invest your time (not requiring you work).

This is wealth measured in time.

For example, if your monthly expenses (debts/liabilities) come to £1,000 each month and you have a secure asset portfolio that produces £1,200 in net income each month without necessitating you invest your time, each month you have a £200 net balance after paying off expenses. Unless some major disaster occurs (and providing that your income is continuous and exceeds your expenses), you will be financially free because your wealth is infinite. On the other hand, if you have a net worth of £100,000 in an investment or in an asset with no passive income producing ability, *this is wealth measured in money alone*. Net worth that can't be converted into cash flow is of little or no value. Once your asset is liquidated you will be 100 months (8.4 years) wealthy.

This is wealth measured in money.

A lot of people fail to gain financial freedom because they're trying to become wealthy via the *money path* alone and they focus on increasing their net worth by trying to accumulate (save or invest) enough money or non-income producing assets so they can retire or not have to worry about working again. This is the slow path towards becoming financially free. The fastest path to financial freedom is through the *time* not the *money* path. First your focus should be to get out of the rat race by setting yourself free, and then with your newfound freedom you will be able to channel your resources towards building more wealth and increasing your net worth.

This is the path I chose and it works.

Myth 3: You don't have to wait until you're old and worn out to be financially free. Retirement has little to do with achieving financial freedom, and most retired people aren't financially free. My father and I retired from our engineering professions within two months of each other. He was sixty-five and I was thirty-three, but the difference was that I had bought back thirty-two years of my life by retiring early. This afforded me the opportunity to review my past and (more importantly) my future and how I wanted to spend the rest of my life. Too many people have been programmed into the mindset of becoming an employee and working for money for their whole life so they can retire on a rocking chair. Instead of pursuing the entrepreneurial path by letting money work for them, they trade their health for wealth only to find that later in life they don't have the health to enjoy what they worked so hard to acquire.

Retiring early allowed me to move into the second phase of my life – the path of purpose, passion and freedom. Time isn't the main factor in achieving financial freedom – your plan is. You don't have to work until you're sixty-five to be financially free. You don't need to work for money for your entire life to be free. You can become financially free within ten years by following the ideas and strategies outlined in this book.

CHAPTER 5

START WITHIN:
HIDDEN SECRETS

We only see what we want to see; we only hear what we want to hear. Our belief system is just like a mirror that only shows us what we believe.

— Don Miguel Ruiz

Understanding the rules and myths of wealth is important, but to change your financial life, you need the right philosophies and beliefs. Wealth is a product of your thinking, and your thinking is hugely influenced by your philosophies and beliefs. We are generally protective about our philosophies and beliefs, even when there's overwhelming evidence they aren't helping us to produce the results we want. We protect them because we believe they are an intricate part of our identity.

For many years, I adopted a poverty philosophy, and although it wasn't helping me I anesthetised the pain because it gave me comfort. It wasn't until I started to change my philosophy and attitude that I began to notice changes in my life. In truth, I needed a complete attitude overhaul.

Your attitude is a habit of thought, and if you want to change your attitude, you must change the way you think. You are where you are in

23

life because of the thoughts that have dominated your mind. To get you to where you want to be, you need the right thoughts.

Maxwell Maltz, the American cosmetic surgeon and author, made a breakthrough in human physiology when he discovered that our self-image is the overriding factor for who we become. He had carried out a number of successful cosmetic surgeries for people in the hope that it would make them see and feel better about themselves, but to his surprise their behaviour and character remained unchanged because of the image (past picture) they had of themselves. These patients had internalised pictures of themselves with their past deformities and physical scars. Although surgery fixed the external defects, it didn't heal them internally. Your success or lack of it hinges on the picture you have of you – your self-image.

To become wealthy you must start within, not without – you need a positive, healthy self-image. You must have an accurate and positive view of yourself before you set your goal to be financially free or you will be held back by your limiting beliefs. If you have an unhealthy or poor self-image, the effort, energy and time you invest will be in vain.

Our beliefs have a strong influence on who we become. Beliefs precede performance, and to get the results you want in your life, you have to start with your beliefs. The right ones will help you take better action and ultimately produce better results. Below are some of the wealth philosophies and beliefs you have to internalise and adopt so you have the right foundation to build your financial future. Each of them is important because during the tough times your physiological stamina and emotional fitness will keep you going.

Income creates security but profit makes you wealthy: If you work for an income, the company you work for decides your value. If you work for profit, you decide what your value is and the level of compensation you receive. No matter how much you earn from your job, it will rarely make you wealthy. If you want to be wealthy, change your mindset and work to acquire investment assets that produce a profit instead of simply staying in a job that pays you a salary. An income will make you a living; investment assets will make you wealthy.

If you depend on an income, what you earn will be limited. If you work for profit there is no limit except that which you decide for yourself. Work for an income and you will increase your wealth incrementally; work for profit and you will increase your wealth exponentially.

Wealth is created in your spare time: Everyone can become wealthy because wealth is created by how much time you allocate towards activities that create opportunities for building wealth, and you can do this during your spare time even if you have a full-time job. To be wealthy, you need to earn and invest simultaneously – and this requires that you become an intelligent investor. You can develop the skills, wisdom and abilities you need first by study and then by practice. It's best to do this during your spare time. Rather than spending your spare time on entertainment and relaxation alone, you should allocate one or two hours daily towards activities that will help you to achieve your financial dreams.

Don't work for money; instead have money work for you: The wealthy work for investment assets, not money or income: To be wealthy you must have money work for you by acquiring investment income producing assets. I was taught to work hard for money, and I did this until I understood that the purpose of working for money was simply to learn the necessary discipline and wisdom I needed so money would work for me. Your focus must be on reversing the role once you start accumulating money. There is a finite amount of energy, effort and time you can invest in working for money, and if you work for money, you won't get wealthy. You have to learn to work harder on yourself than you do for money. First, work to develop the skills, knowledge and wisdom you need, and then use that wisdom to create investment assets that work for you. Never work solely for a pay cheque.

If you shift your thinking from the notion that you're working for a pay cheque to one founded on the philosophy that you are working to acquire income producing assets, half of your work is already done. The trouble is that many people can't see beyond the money trap. Wealth is created by working to acquire assets and putting those assets to work so they create money for you every day. By changing your employer from money to assets, you change your life. The ultimate key to financial freedom lies in having multiple income streams. Choose to work for assets not money.

Create multiple sources of investment income: You need multiple income streams to create, grow and maintain wealth. This is the source of wealth and riches – not a job or having more than one job. Your income can come from a variety of passive (from investments) sources that don't demand much of your time or energy unlike active income (from a job). Start with earned income if necessary, but invest some of your earned income in assets that create investment income, then reinvest the generated income in another income stream. Keep doing this until you have a strong portfolio of investments that produce continuous income even whilst you sleep. Money will make you a living if you work for it, but investment assets make you wealthy. Learn to have money (assets) work for you instead of slaving for it. Invest your time in creating a product or service (an asset) that can produce investment income for you whether you work or not – and preferably assets that demand little of your time and energy to manage them.

Financial ignorance causes financial poverty: If you want to be wealthy, you must be financially literate. Financial intelligence isn't the same as academic or professional education. You can be professionally competent and technically sound but still financially illiterate. Your financial intelligence will help you solve your financial problems and also see opportunities. Money alone doesn't make you wealthy; what you know does. You need good judgement, understanding, and wisdom. Wealth is a product of your understanding and how you apply your knowledge towards your pre-determined financial objective. To become wealthy you need financial education in the use of taxes, debt, trends, history, economics and accounting. This knowledge will empower you with the ability to resolve financial problems and identify wealth opportunities. Wisdom provides a quicker path to financial freedom when compared to learning from personal experience alone and requires daily investment in your mind.

Liabilities keep you poor; assets make you wealthy: All investments are not created equal. One of the biggest mistakes we make is in assuming all investments are good. Noting can be further from the truth. There are good and bad investments, and similarly there are good and bad assets, and there are good and bad liabilities. Good assets make you wealthy; bad liabilities make you poor. Any investment that necessities the flow of cash from you towards the asset rather than the other way around is a bad asset. For example, your home is a good investment (it could help you increase your net worth), but it's a bad asset if it's mortgaged because it causes cash to flow (mortgage, insurance, maintenance) away from you rather than towards you each month. The key to wealth is to acquire good investments – good assets – and minimise bad assets or liabilities. One strategy used by the rich is to purchase good investment assets first and use the income generated by them to cover any liabilities (home, car, boats, planes).

Wealth has a unique language: Wealth has its own vocabulary. Learn it, practice it and soon you'll speak it. Your words change the way you think, and the quality of your thoughts decides your character and your destiny. Education combined with vision, wisdom and hard work will make you wealthy. Make a study of wealth if you wish to be wealthy. Your vocabulary starts with understanding the four basic wealth words – assets, liabilities, cash flow and leverage.

Your wealth is determined by how cash flows into or out of your life. Many people confuse the words *assets* and *liabilities* and few understand the importance of cash flow and leverage in building wealth. To become wealthy, upgrade your vocabulary, learn the language of money and become fluent so you can identify opportunities, communicate effectively and take advantage of the wealth strategies utilised by the wealthy.

Income (money) doesn't make you wealthy. What you do with your income does: We all work for two main income sources – earned (active) and investment (passive or portfolio) income. (Earned income is the income you work for and investment income is the income you obtain by having money work for you.) To be wealthy, you have to make the right decisions about what to do with what you earn. The average person works hard for earned income but they have a lifestyle that repels wealth. It doesn't matter how much you earn if you have no discipline and spend all you earn each month – you won't become wealthy. Many are unable to live within their means, despite earning a reasonable wage, and each month they have little or nothing to invest and they remain financially dependent. Wealthy people invest their money first and then spend what's left. The average person spends their money first

27

and then save what's left – and in most cases there's nothing available to invest. The amount you earn can be irrelevant without discipline and sound financial habits.

Saving won't make you wealthy; investing will: Stop focusing on saving – focus instead on investing. Saving for the long term is an obsolete idea in terms of wealth creation. You passively save to invest; you don't actively save to become wealthy. To become wealthy, discard your saving lifestyle and become an investor. Your money needs to be put to good use. You can't work and save your way to financial freedom and still have the health, time and energy to enjoy that freedom. Saving and investing require almost the same amount of effort, but investing uses the compounding principle – generating earnings from previous earnings through continuous reinvestment of the original capital and interest earned. You can't save your way into wealth but you can invest your way to wealth. The purchasing power of a currency generally tends to decline. As the government prints money, this devalues the currency so any money saved in a currency form today will be worth less in the future, meaning that saving money for the long term isn't wise. Most people save in a currency, but money isn't the only currency – gold and silver are forms of currency but they don't de-value at the same rate as money. They're both finite, unlike money that can be reprinted. Both are better alternatives in terms of protecting your currency for the long term if your preference is to save. But if you're trying to save your way to wealth, you don't stand a chance if you use money alone. If you must save for the long term, change the currency.

Wealth is created through long not short term thinking: Poverty and lack are products of thinking from day to day and week to week, but abundance and freedom comes from thinking from decade to decade. If you want to be wealthy, think long term and dismiss invitations to focus on the present (today or tomorrow). This could be difficult for those on a limited income, but it is doable. Your ability to stretch your thinking into the future will decide how quickly you become financially free. The longevity of your thinking process determines whether you focus on survival, comfort or freedom. Thinking short term is usually influenced by the scarcity mindset, but long term thinking is influenced by the abundance mindset. The abundance mindset leads to freedom; the survival mindset attracts security. This means that your decisions and actions shouldn't be about instant gratification but instead you should focus on the best long term decisions. You must think long term when investing – the key is usually to keep things simple, and invest smartly and for the long term.

Become a life goal setter: Goals hold the key to success and provide a means for turning dreams into reality. Your ability to set goals and successfully follow through with the necessary sacrifices to make them reality is how wealth is created. One of the most important reasons for setting a goal (especially to be financially free) is to see what it will make of you to achieve it. Who you become in pursuit of or during the progressive realisation of your goal is what matters the most – someone with more wisdom, skills and abilities. The ultimate path to wealth lies in developing the discipline to set and achieve your life goals – not short, medium or long term goals, but *life goals.*

We often overestimate what we can achieve in one year but underestimate what we can achieve in ten years. Focus on your future ten, fifteen, thirty and forty years from today when choosing your financial goals.

Think about ideas, problems to solve and where you can add value to others: Ideas provide solutions to problems, and your financial wealth will be in proportion to the problems you solve for others, but more importantly the value you create in the process. Wealthy people are obsessed with finding new ideas to solve problems, and to become wealthy you should spend less time on thinking and talking about things or people and instead focus on how you can resolve problems and create value for others. How you use your time determines how wealthy you become.

Your thoughts control your focus and where your energy is directed. What do you think and talk about – ideas, things or people? Your answer determines whether you fall into the group that makes things happen, the group that stands back and watches things happen, or if you're one of the many who talk about the people who make things happen. You have to be constantly creative, solve more problems, and add tremendous value for others to remain wealthy. You have to use your imagination on a daily basis to look for ways to create value for others by solving problems for them. You have to think creatively, because ideas are seeds for the harvest of riches.

Money doesn't make money. The right ideas and the right solutions to problems create wealth.

Questions hold the key to riches so ask intelligently: Asking empowering questions is one of the important traits of the wealthy. It was one question asked properly and timely that made a dropout college student the richest man in the world. I'm talking about Bill Gates, who was brave enough to ask, 'How can we (Microsoft) become the intelligence that supports all computers and businesses in the world?' This question made him the richest (financially) person in the world and has kept him in the same position for eighteen out of the past twenty-three years. All life's answers (especially those that will make you wealthy) are hidden in questions. The quality of the questions you ask determines the answers you get. This is because your questions control your thinking (and vice versa), and your thoughts control your focus and energy which in turn decide your feelings, actions and results. If you ask empowering questions, you will get empowering answers – and the opposite is true. Money is attracted to those who seek it diligently.

CHAPTER 6

WEALTH SORES: CHANGE OLD PARADIGMS, CHANGE YOUR LIFE

The great enemy of the truth is very often not the lie, deliberate, contrived and dishonest, but the myth, persistent, persuasive and unrealistic.
— *John F. Kennedy*

Everything we do is either in pursuit of a gain or to avoid pain, and the same applies to how most people react to wealth and money. Although people might say they want to be financially free, their actions (what they do and how they live) aren't consistent with their desires. This is often because their desire for wealth is stuck at a conscious level and hasn't moved into their subconscious mind which controls their behaviour and actions. Unfortunately, some people subconsciously associate negative feelings with money and often act in ways contrary to what they want. It's like the story of Daisy the cow, who after producing beautiful milk raised her legs and kicked the bucket, spilling the milk she produced. People work to acquire money but their subconscious mind works just as hard to keep money away from them because of the negative ideas and associations they have about money.

It's important that you take some time for self-analysis to understand if and why you have any negative conditioning towards money. To help you with this, let's look at some of the reasons people keep themselves from having money. Do you have any of these negative subconscious beliefs?

- I would have to sacrifice who I am and my family to get it
- It's reserved for a select few – the really smart ones
- I'd need to compromise on my beliefs or values
- Money won't make me happy
- I may lose the important things in my life that mean a lot to me
- It's reserved for a select few – the really smart ones
- There's only a limited amount available for everyone so I'd have to steal it from someone else

These misinterpretations and feelings of guilt result in people remaining in lack, and they don't make financial freedom a goal. They have an unconscious way of sabotaging themselves as soon as they start making any progress. Self-sabotage is when we say we want something and go about making sure it doesn't happen. Many people self-sabotage on a daily basis. I had this problem for years. Being raised poor limited and blinded me to the truth. I had internalised some false beliefs, and through combining those with some incorrect interpretations of Biblical scripture, I remained in lack.

There are two distinct views about money. One is that wealth and prosperity is a materialistic way to live and should be shunned, and at the other is the view that prosperity is good and something we should all aspire to have.

Growing up, I recall hearing references to money such as:

- God must love poor people because he created so many of them

- It is easier for a camel to go through the eye of a needle than for someone who is rich to enter the kingdom of God
- Money is the root of all evil
- If God wants you to have it, he will give it to you.

A lot of people quote verses from the Bible that suggest money is something bad but I seldom hear people quote, *Money is the answer for everything* (Ecclesiastes 10:19) said by King Solomon of ancient Israel who is regarded as the wisest and richest man who ever lived. Your experiences might be different from mine; they might not have been in a religious context. Your attitude towards wealth could have come from some of the common limiting beliefs that have kept other individuals, families, businesses and countries in lack, such as:

- Money doesn't grow on trees
- The rich are greedy
- Money is not that important and it isn't everything
- Money is there to be spent
- The rich get richer and the poor get poorer
- I'm not good with money
- Money is a limited resource and available to a select few
- You have to work (too) hard to get money
- Only selfish people want a lot of money

As a result of these false philosophies, beliefs and limiting words, I subconsciously associated more pain with acquiring money than not having it, and it wasn't until I decided to invest time in educating myself about money and wealth that I was able to break my reoccurring pattern of self-sabotage.

Ignorance is (in my opinion) the greatest tragedy in the world – wars are fought, people are killed, destinies are stolen, greatness remains unseen, poverty is embraced, and many remain poor – all because of ignorance. It was the prevalence of ignorance that led one ancient writer to say, *My people are destroyed from lack of knowledge* (Hosea 4:6).

The emotional attachment we have towards money plays a vital role in our financial lives. Some of our emotions stem from our beliefs, philosophies and our experiences (good, bad or ugly). Some people fail to achieve financial freedom because of the emotional scars they have about money. Interestingly, your experience with money says more about you than it does about money. Money is just money – it's neutral, although it's also a magnifier and makes you more of whoever you are.

If you self sabotage, don't worry, because there is a way out. You can overcome this by ridding yourself of your old habits or patterns of thinking. The place to start is by changing your beliefs about money and wealth, and you can achieve this by replacing your negative beliefs with more positive and empowering beliefs about money. More importantly, you can replace false beliefs with the truth – only the truth can set you free.

Let us start by identifying some empowering thoughts to help you recondition your thoughts and beliefs.

- Money is a reward for creating value and solving problems for others
- Money is a force for doing good in the world and can be used to create memorable experiences for myself and others
- Making and earning money is my obligation, responsibility and duty
- There is an abundance of money for everyone who seeks it
- Money is attracted to me and therefore it serves me
- I respect money but I don't love it
- I have money but it doesn't have me
- Money can help me fulfil my purpose

Spaced repetition is an effective way of developing a new attitude about wealth. That means that these new empowering affirmations about money should be repeated on a daily basis until you start to see changes in your attitude towards money.

A new attitude

All your experiences are fed to your subconscious mind, and your attitudes and self-image are formed from these inputs. Unlike a computer hard drive that can be formatted or completely replaced, it isn't possible to simply erase your past inputs – neither is it necessary. You can't rid yourself of a thought, because your mind moves toward a currently dominant thought, but you can replace one thought with another. To change your philosophy and beliefs about wealth, you need new inputs to change your attitudes and condition your mind towards wealth.

This requires four steps – the right inputs, processing the inputs, positive reinforcement through space repetition, and action. To change your attitude towards wealth, you need to make a conscious choice to change. Until you're completely certain you want to change, your efforts will be in vain.

You must change what you sow if you want a different harvest. If you:

- Sow a thought, you reap a feeling
- Sow a feeling, you reap an action
- Sow an action, you reap a habit
- Sow a habit you reap a character
- Sow a character, you reap a destiny

Change your thoughts and you can change your life.

CHAPTER 7

FOUR PILLARS: SECURING YOUR FINANCIAL FUTURE

Rule number one: Don't lose money. Rule number two:
Don't forget rule number one.

— *Warren Buffett*

There's no mystery to wealth; it is simply the result of obeying principles, rules and laws. Life functions according to laws (for example, the laws of energy and gravity), and it's reasonable to assume that there are specific wealth principles, laws and rules that will guarantee the promised outcomes when applied. And one of the most important things to do in any area of life is to find out how things work before you start.

There are some basic principles upon which wealth is built. These principles go back as far as time began and don't need to be changed. Wealth must be built on a strong foundation for it to last, and the principles we will soon discuss form the four pillars of wealth. To begin your wealth journey, you should ask, *What things will create the results I want?*

Financial wealth is a science, and like in any branch of science there are laws and principles that govern its creation, multiplication and protection. Once these are mastered, good results are guaranteed with absolute certainty – if the principles are followed. Wealth isn't a matter of environment; some environments are more favourable than others, but wealth is created by doing things in a certain way. This ability isn't down to talent or IQ.

There are more people achieving financial freedom every day than ever before. The Forbes Billionaire 2017 list states that the number of billionaires increased by 233 (a thirteen per cent rise) in 2016, the biggest in the thirty-one years that Forbes has been tracking billionaires globally. The question isn't 'can you'; it's 'will you'? If others can do it, you can.

To have something you don't have, you have to become someone you aren't. This is true in all areas of life and even more so in the area of wealth. The road to financial freedom is a narrow and bumpy one, but the journey can be a remarkable experience if you apply the right principles, philosophy and attitude. Wealth creation like success is the willingness to bear pain – the willingness to do consistently what others won't for the promise that few will experience. But the burden of pain can only be endured if the promise of the future is beautifully painted. Your duty is to paint the picture of the promise so beautifully that you are willing to pay the price.

There are four core pillars upon which financial dreams are built – planning, discipline, budgeting, and patience.

Planning

Financial freedom starts with a plan and is maintained by following a plan. Without a well written, regularly reviewed and vigorously executed plan, you will remain poor. You need a plan and a strategy on how to secure, protect, increase, and share wealth. Income doesn't create wealth; making more money will not create wealth until you do something with the income you earn. To retire young and wealthy, you need a plan. There are various vehicles you can use to achieve financial freedom, but at the core are four major investment paths – business, property, commodities and paper assets (stocks, bonds, mutual funds, etc.). None of these vehicles is effective without a plan. Wealth is created and sustained as a result of your plan, not because of your chosen investment product, strategy or vehicle.

There are three distinct components of a good wealth plan –the first is *protection*, the second your *safety and security* plan, and the third is *investing*. Irrespective of where you are financially, you should begin with your protection plan. Protection is critically important when trying to build wealth because it covers the unexpected, such as major liabilities relating to health, business or wealth, and the best way to prepare for this is through insurance (life insurance, critical illness, asset protection, personal liability or public liability insurance). This should be a consideration, especially if you have a business, family or dependants.

The second is the safe and secure component and this ensures you have a safety cushion in your life. There are two parts to this plan – the present and future. Your safety plan for the present is achieved through short term active saving through an emergency saving fund. Your safety plan for the future is achieved by passive saving for the long term through a pre-tax pension scheme. A pension scheme is a savings plan, not an investment plan. It will help you stay secure, but it won't make you wealthy. If you choose to save in a pension, you should think wisely about your contributions. Your focus should be to passively save and actively invest.

With your protection and safety plan in place, you can begin your investment plan, which is where investment strategies and vehicles for increasing wealth are essential. Investing is where wealth is created, multiplied and leveraged, and it requires choosing the right investment strategies and vehicles that can generate multiples sources of income for you. We'll discuss this in detail in later chapters.

Discipline

The ability to make yourself do what needs to be done in the present and in the appropriate manner (irrespective of your feelings) to ensure that your desires for the future can be realised is discipline in action. The discipline you exercise should be based on your vision of freedom, and the strength of your discipline will mirror the clarity, passion and desire behind your vision.

Discipline begins with where you are and what you have, and the key is to sustaining the level of discipline you need to be financially free lies in developing daily habits and routines which mirror your goals. The wealthy aren't smarter or more intelligent than you; they simply discipline themselves to do things differently because they have developed habits, rituals and routines which they practice without fail. Self-discipline is a prerequisite to wealth, and it requires that you control and direct your emotions, desires, behaviour, and actions in the present so they're in alignment with what you want from your future.

The importance of discipline can't be over-emphasised in the wealth journey. Without discipline, there's no hope. Some of the most forms of discipline you will need to build the right foundation for wealth include the disciplines of:

- Spending less than you earn
- Compulsive investing
- Keeping accurate financial accounts
- Paying yourself first
- Delayed gratification
- Focus
- Good wealth habits
- Continuous learning
- Effective management

Sacrifice

If you are going to become wealthy and free, something has to give. You need to sacrifice your time, energy, instant gratification, and yourself. Sacrifice comes in two parts – what you have to give up and what you have to do. During the early stages of your journey you might need to sacrifice some time. This could be in the form of time away from family and friends, a reduction in your leisure time, giving up on some sleep or postponing a few holidays. I'm not suggesting what you should sacrifice; that's a matter of personal choice. However, if you intend to be wealthy, you can't put off the inevitable – if you're not willing to make sacrifices, you won't be wealthy. Sacrifice should be tailored in proportion to your dream and should take into account your lifestyle and personal circumstances.

Desire and sacrifice must come together to create wealth. Subtraction comes before multiplication in the wealth equation. You need to give up something of value to gain something else of greater perceived value, and often the price has to be paid on a daily basis.

Budgeting

A budget is an essential tool to effectively manage your financial life, but many people don't keep to one because they're repelled by the thought of depriving themselves of the fun they believe they deserve. Anyone who says you don't need a budget didn't start their wealth journey from the bottom. You start with a budget, but you shouldn't live forever on a budget. If you were raised poor, or raised rich with no concept of the value of time and money, you'll probably have little or no concept of delayed gratification, which means that a budget will irritate you. A budget gives you structure and the opportunity to develop discipline.

A budget is simply a plan. Once you've developed the discipline to stick to the steps in your plan, you'll attract more wealth opportunities. The best gift you get from living from a budget is that it teaches you one of the greatest lessons of life – to be faithful in little things, so you will be faithful in large ones. A budget will help you on your path to financial freedom, but the key is to develop discipline and keep creating more wealth until you arrive at the place where a budget is unnecessary. Without a budget, there's no discipline, and without discipline, you can forget financial freedom.

Patience

It takes time to create wealth. Some say patience is a virtue, but it's also a gift. Patience doesn't guarantee success but it increases your odds if you have good staying power. It is a rare trait in today's world. Every day we're lured into instant gratification and entitlement traps. Our impatience is displayed in two forms. Firstly, our inability to delay gratification and secondly, the lack of patience to wait for results. Wealth isn't a get rich quick process and it isn't created overnight. It takes time.

Instant gratification is often the familiar voice in our heads that gently whispers: *You deserve that nice dress this month. You deserve that expensive car now. You're due for a holiday because you've worked hard. You can put it on your credit card without saving up.*

Patience leads to wealth, but discipline is difficult to practice or promote as we live in a society that doesn't believe that patience has any merit. We live in a culture of now and are encouraged to forget about the future and buy now, spend now.

There's a time for sowing and one for reaping – don't try to do both at the same time. Patience provides the connecting link between both seasons.

Part 3

PAY THE PRICE FOR THE PROMISE

CHAPTER 8

TEN STEPS: DESIGN THE FUTURE

Go forth on your path, as it exists only through your walking.
— Saint Augustine of Hippo

We have discussed some of the important and essential prerequisite steps and knowledge you must have before you begin your journey to wealth. In this chapter, we're going to move from the preparation to the action stage, which begins with crystallising your dream of freedom by giving it permanence in written form as a goal. Your goal is simply a written or documented form of your dream with a timeline on when it should become a reality. Goals are the single biggest contributor to success, and a lack of clearly defined financial goals is one reason why few become wealthy.

Before getting into the goal setting process, it's important that you do two things. First, you need to establish where you are financially. Refer to your financial statement if you have one because it paints a more accurate picture of your current situation. Look at the numbers. They tell a story, and before you can plan the future you need to know where you are. Reviewing your position will highlight your habits and whether you have a poor or wealthy person's lifestyle. Don't

45

get emotional about it; let the numbers reveal the truth. It might be frustrating at first, but it will also set you free. If you don't have a financial statement, don't worry. Later in the book, I'll show you how to prepare one.

Secondly, you have to decide on your destination because your goal is only as effective as the plan you choose. What do you really want – how much money do you need to be free? Do you know, or are you too busy dealing with your daily responsibilities and job to work that out? We often get so busy with earning a living that we forget to design our lives. To be clear about your destination, you need clearly defined goals and objectives.

If you've recently travelled to central London as a tourist, or visited a large shopping centre, you may have found yourself in need of directions. This is where the tourist information centre map becomes invaluable because on that map is a sign that says *You are here*. Once you know your location, and can clearly see your destination, you can recalculate your travel path.

Setting your goals does the same thing – it creates a road map.

To help you define your goals and objectives, answer the following questions:

- What do you want? What are the outcomes or end result you badly want? Your answer to this question will guide your thinking. To become financially free, you must know what you want. Is your goal to be secure, comfortable or rich? What will secure, comfortable or rich look like, and is it quantifiable in monetary terms?

- Why do you want it? (You should already have this figured out by now as we dealt with this earlier). Your goals take on a greater meaning when you know your 'why'. Your why will motivate you.

- Why don't you already have it? What has kept you from achieving your dream before now? If financial freedom is important to you and your family, why isn't it reality? Are there specific skills, resources or abilities you lack and need?

- What are the benefits? What awaits you when you achieve your goal? The benefits provide inspiration and focus and it's important to know what the specific benefits will be.

- How will you measure your success? Most people run a race set by others, so they don't get a sense of completion because they're unclear about what the achieved goal should look like.

- Who will you become when you achieve your goal? It's important to know where your goal will lead you. The most important part of setting a goal to become financially free is so you become the type of person who deserves the goal.

With these six questions answered, you're ready for the goal setting process.

The formula

For the goal-setting process to be successful you have to follow some ground rules. It requires time and patience to complete it successfully. It is about looking into the future, bringing the picture of the future back to the present, and using the picture to inspire you to action.

Step 1: Decide what you want and write it down. Your financial goal must be in writing to start the process. It shouldn't be in your head but in a form where you can see it daily. Clarity is power, so include as much detail as you can and remember that you are allowing yourself to dream and are writing by faith and vision (what you desire) not by sight (what is currently possible). The more specific you are about what you want, the faster your brain, mind and heart will get you there. Faith requires precision to work; you must know exactly what you want. Assume that there are no restrictions to what you can have. It may seem that you need a magic wand – so be it.

Remember that financial freedom is arriving at a place where you no longer have to work for necessities (but you can choose to if you wish), and is achieved when the income from your investments exceeds the expenses you need to maintain your current lifestyle. There are three things you must do at this stage:

1) Fix the exact amount you want in your mind.

2) Identify the type of investments you want and how much would you want each investment to generate as income.

3) Decide how much money in surplus each month you need to cover any unforeseen issues (what income/expense ratio you want to have).

Step 2: Set a deadline by assigning a timeframe for achieving your goal. To aim for financial freedom without clarity of timing is to push yourself back into the zone of wishing, thinking and fantasising, and away from objective and determined planning. You must take time to carefully evaluate your ultimate date for reaching your goal – this should take into account your age, income, personal liabilities and expenses, the projected economic and political climate, the available opportunities you have studied and evaluated, social trends, and market conditions. Each goal requires a timeline – financial freedom is no different.

Make a realistic assessment of how long you believe it will take to achieve your goal.

Remember that success is the joy that comes from journey towards your intended goal. The keyword here is *joy*. With that in mind, remember that any goal or desire you are pursuing that robs you of your joy in life isn't worth having. There should be joy even in discipline and sacrifice because you're working for a greater reward. But if the timeline you choose is unrealistic, you will place unnecessary pressure and stress on yourself and this will rob you of all joy and happiness. Be wise in choosing your deadline.

Step 3: Identify and document five reasons why you want to achieve each your goal. Your goal will draw you into the future if it's clearly defined and the reasons behind it are strong. Reasons are the fuel for goal achievement, and without a strong enough reason it's impossible to persevere. Your reason identifies the 'why' for wanting the goal, and when the 'why' is clear and strong, it helps you see the 'how.' Now is the time to crystallise your personal reasons on paper if you didn't write them down earlier.

Step 4: Identify and document five reasons why you don't have it already. If you aren't financially free already, there are reasons. Write them down. The purpose is not so you can transfer the blame or play the victim card; it's so you know what to focus on. Is it:

- Lack of wisdom or financial intelligence?
- Skills you don't have?
- Time you don't have due to other personal commitments?
- A character or an ability issue?
- An income or debt issue?
- Self-image or self -belief issue?

What is it? Write it down. Remember, you are the most important part of the equation. My experience has led me to believe that ninety per cent of the problem lies within (it is often mental and dependent on your psychology) and ten per cent without (strategy). This means you must work on yourself first (your self-image, thoughts, beliefs, philosophy) before attempting to change any external part of you.

All financial freedom goals can be achieved by four distinct factors: time factor, ability, desire and drive – opportunity or lack thereof.

Step 5: Determine the price you have to pay or what you have to give up to achieve your goal. Financial freedom requires sacrifice. The biggest sacrifice will be letting go of who you are today – your habits, lifestyle and thinking pattern – to become someone with the improved character who deserves to achieve your goal. Also, what sacrifices will you need to make in the other areas of your life – relationships (time with family and friends), health, career and business, socially? And how will your sacrifices affect your priorities?

Step 6: Plan out the problems. Financial freedom is a major goal, and like all major and long term goals it will come with a host of problems which will require your attention. Your victory over the problems will depend on whether you react or respond to them. Reaction occurs as a result of lack of planning; responding on the other hand comes from a place of peace and calm due to proper planning and preparation. The biggest mistake most people make is that they believe their journey will be smooth and problem-free, and as soon as they're faced with a major problem they are knocked off focus and don't resume their journey. You should plan out the problem areas before you begin your journey, because things you don't plan for *will* come up.

Step 7: Create a plan and a strategy for achieving your goal. Financial freedom isn't something you stumble into – it's a product of a well-developed plan and a vigorously executed strategy, and you must convert your goals into a plan. Choose your plan for wealth creation, multiplication, budgeting, investing, protection and sharing. Most people hope that the future will get better, but the future doesn't get better through hope; it gets better by planning. If you are hoping alone without a plan, you're certain to have a disappointing future. Your success and the achievement of your goal hinges on your plan.

Step 8: Connect your goals to a greater purpose or life contribution. A goal connected to a greater purpose (such as improving the lives of others) provides an incredible source of energy and passion towards attaining your goal. For example, your reason for wanting to become wealthy could be so you can help your local church or your favourite charity. The goal of Andrew Carnegie, the Scottish-American industrialist and philanthropist, was to become wealthy in the first half of his life so he could spend the rest of his life investing his wealth in the lives of others. As a result of connecting his goal to a greater purpose, he became one of the wealthiest men ever. He gave away almost ninety per cent of his wealth (approximately $80 billion in today's terms) to charities, foundations and universities. Imagine how your goal could be expanded and achieved if you connected it to a greater cause.

Step 9: Convert your goal to daily habits. With your financial goal, plan and strategy documented, begin with the end in mind and work backwards from the future to the present. Break your goals into smaller objectives and into daily habits and routines that (if practiced daily) will get you to your goal. Daily habits and routine form one of the secrets to success. Your life is hidden in a day, and a day is hidden in life. What you do daily decides who you become permanently. Instead of focusing on your future success, focus on making one day successful and repeat it. To achieve this, you need new wealth habits which you live every day.

Step 10: Schedule your review and recovery moments. Once you've finalised your goal, you will quickly recognise how much is involved, and you must plan and schedule moments for review, rest, recovery and restitution. One of the most common reasons why people don't achieve their goals is burnout and fatigue. We understand this in sports, and even in our jobs, but most people ignore the idea when it comes to their life. You should schedule daily, monthly, quarterly and yearly time slots to review your progress, but more importantly to rest and renew your mind, body, and spirit. Yes, you want to be financially free, but the process should be fun. Don't burn yourself out trying to gain wealth at the sacrifice of your health, relationships, emotion and joy. Don't exhaust yourself so when you achieve your goal you can't enjoy it.

You will also need to review your progress regularly because this is often the key to becoming wealthy and free. Do this once a week and at the end of the month. I personally like to review and rewrite my goals twice a day – first thing in the morning and in the evening just before going to bed – and I use the evening review as an opportunity to review my progress for the day.

CHAPTER 9

SQUARE BOXES: MAKE THE GAME WINNABLE

Your net worth to the world is usually determined by what remains after your bad habits are subtracted from your good ones.

— Benjamin Franklin

Wealth is a product of the allocation of resources not the availability of opportunity alone. You need awareness on your wealth journey as it enables you to successfully allocate resources and identify opportunities. You have decided on your intended destination but in order to plan out the best route or vehicle you need to know your present location – where you are. Being in the right place at the right time is good, but without awareness, you're none the wiser. In the previous chapter, we discussed how to choose your destination, but this is where the rubber meets the road. It's time to get real and you need to start by assessing your personal finances. Stretch yourself if you wish, get yourself a drink, a journal or paper, a pen and a calculator. We're going to prepare your financial and wealth statement so you can understand where you are, and also create a strategy and a plan to get you financially free.

Financial statement

On the first page in your journal write 'financial statement' and today's date. Below this draw a square and split it into two equal halves to create four square boxes. In each box write the following: income, expenses, assets, liabilities. On the next page of your journal write 'income', on the following page write 'expenses' and then on the next two pages write 'liabilities/debts' and 'assets'. Let's look at each part of your financial statement in more detail:

Income: On your income page, make a list of your income sources. When you've done this, write next to each income source the amount you receive – monthly or annually. This should be your net not gross income. (Your gross income is the amount of salary or wages paid to you by your employer before any deductions and your net income is the residual amount after deductions such as taxes and pension contributions). In addition to your regular income, include investment income or any income from other sources. Try not to overestimate or exaggerate the amount. This list is yours and you don't need to try to impress anyone. When you've identified all the income amounts, add them up to obtain your *net income* (monthly and yearly).

Expenses: Make a list of your expenses each month. Your bank or credit card statements will make it easier to extract the information. All cash transactions also need to be identified and documented. Your expenses should include your routine and non-routine items. For example, your routine items might include mortgage or rent, and insurance. Non-routine expenses could include food, clothing, travel, utilities, gym or club memberships, estimated social expenses, personal grooming and other living expenses. Write down the actual amount spent each month (or year) next to each item. If you don't have the actual amount for a particular item, make an educated guess of what it might be from the month's statement. Add up the figures to get the total sum. Next add ten per cent to the total amount to get your *estimated total expenses*. The reason for the extra ten per cent is that we tend to underestimate how much is really owed and often omit (perhaps unintentionally) one or two items. Also, sometimes we don't include some of the hidden charges linked with some debts

Liabilities: We've kept your liabilities separate from your expenses for reasons that will be evident shortly. Your liabilities are often payments you hope to stop paying at some point (except where these are investment debts contributing towards your wealth plan) unlike your general expenses which are part of your needs and necessities.

Your liabilities are usually a combination of bad liabilities and some investments. They should include your investment debts such as any loans or mortgages taken out for an investment (include in the income section any passive income you receive). Your liabilities should also include loans – mortgages, home, credit and store cards, car loans, and personal loans. You have to be completely honest here; you can't afford to leave anything hidden. If you need to do this alone rather than with your family, that's OK too. But remember, nothing concealed stays hidden forever, especially debt.

Just like you did with your expenses, make a list of your liabilities and debts and the actual money owed associated with each item. For loans and credit cards, this should include the total balance owed including the monthly minimum payment.

Once you've finished, add it up to get the total sum. Next, add ten per cent to the total amount (like you did for your expenses) to get your *estimated total liabilities*.

The expense and liabilities column of your financial statement identifies your spending habits. Habits make you rich or poor. Study your expenses and you'll see the writing on the wall.

The best way to identify your expenses and liabilities is to monitor and track every penny you spend for a thirty day period. But don't put the planning process on hold. Instead, do both simultaneously, and once you've finished the thirty day exercise you can make any necessary corrections. What you will find valuable from this tracking exercise is the awareness it brings of your spending habits. Your financial journey will become easier because you will know where the leak in your income bucket is and you then can fix it.

Assets: Write down your assets – good (investment assets that generate an income) and bad assets (investment assets that have an expense monthly or no reoccurring expense). At this point, discount any assets that aren't under your complete control such as potential assets promised in a will, a promissory note, or those that will be yours sometime in the future when you've completed the terms of the trade. Your asset list should include everything you own – gadgets, equipment/tools, jewellery, businesses, property, paper assets (stocks, bonds) and commodities. Include everything – small or large. Next to each item add the value of each of the items, not their aspirational value, but their current market value. Approach this task in two parts – for investment assets assume that you have to sell all your possessions within a week and use the current market value. For personal effects and items such as cars and jewellery, use the average price from the top five sites in your local area where similar products are bought and sold.

Once you have finished, add it up to get the total sum. Next, deduct fifteen per cent from the total amount to get your *estimated present asset worth*. We usually overestimate on the positive side with our assets because we are thinking emotively, but you must remain objective. If you had to sell everything you owned within seven days, you might get only eighty or ninety per cent of your estimated value (especially for your personal items).

Net worth: Add up your total expenses and liabilities and subtract this amount from your present asset worth. *This is your net worth.*

This is a good time to compare your true net worth with your expected net worth to see if you're where you should be financially or if you're falling behind. According to Thomas Stanley's wealth equation, your expected net worth should be ten per cent of your age multiplied by your annual realised household income (10% x age x income = expected net worth). Calculate your expected net worth and compare your expected net worth with your true net worth to ascertain where you stand.

Don't be alarmed by the difference between your current net worth and your expected net worth. It isn't where you start or who you are today that matters. What matters is who you will become and where you're going. Keep your focus on your dream, not the present, even if your net worth is in the negative. A negative net worth is indicative that you spend more money than you make which can be corrected in two ways – earn more (offence strategy which the wealthy follow) and spend less (defence strategy, which is the alternative but also effective approach).

Your net worth doesn't limit you from becoming financially free. Wealth is measured in money (or income) as a function of time not money alone, and having a regular source of cash flow through investment income is the true decider. Your net worth (in assets) means nothing except if you are intending to liquidate some of your assets or convert it into cash flow.

Wealth statement

The primary purpose of your wealth statement is to identify if you're financially free, and if not what you need to get you there. Let's go back to your journal. On a new page write 'wealth statement' and today's date. Below this, draw a big square and split it into two equal halves to create two square boxes. In each write the following; 'investment income' and 'expenses'. This represents important parts of your wealth statement. On a new page on your journal write 'wealth income'.

Wealth income: Make a list of the income producing investments you own. This list should include income you receive through investments alone (passive and portfolio income) and not a job (active income) where you have to exchange your time, energy and presence for it. This could be income from commodities, property, stocks, royalties, businesses, bonds or similar income generating assets.

Don't include any equity from your assets; what we want here is income only – produced from your investment assets. Assets that don't create income are discounted from this part of the wealth calculation process. Although you may have assets with equity that could appreciate in value, you don't intend to sell them so they have to be discounted. Until you choose to sell them they're of no immediate use because their equity is frozen. A cooked meal in the freezer is of no use to you if you're hungry and need to eat immediately; it becomes valuable when defrosted and brought to an edible temperature. Similarly, you can have millions in an asset, but until it creates or produces income, or is converted to money, it does nothing to change your financial position in the present.

Next to each item, add the net amount received daily, monthly or yearly as income (net).

Add up the total amount and you have your estimated total wealth income.

On the next page, write down 'expenses'.

Expenses: You will need to refer back to the expenses and liabilities sections of your financial statement page at this point because you will need to copy over some of the items you listed there. First, copy across your expenses and the amounts. Next copy over the liabilities (those that cause cash flow away from you as an expense) you identified in the liabilities page of your financial statement. You need to focus on cash flowing from you each month (or year) to the respective assets or debts such as an investment debt, a car loan, a mortgage, a student loan or credit card monthly repayment amount.

The purpose of this exercise is to find the total sum you spend each month on your personal expenses and your liabilities, not the total amount owed. For example, if you have a mortgage with a loan amount of £200,000 and a monthly payment of £1,000, then for the wealth assessment, we disregard the £200,000 but we use the monthly £1,000.

Add up your personal expenses and liabilities to get your total wealth expenses.

Wealth worth:
Method 1: To work out your current wealth worth, and see if you're financially free, subtract your total wealth expenses from your total wealth income. If you're left with a net positive amount, the income you receive from your investments exceeds your expenses and therefore you can maintain your current lifestyle without having to work.

Next, divide your income amount by the expenses amount to get your income/expense (wealth) ratio. If this value is greater than one, you're financially free – the higher the ratio, the wealthier you are. This means you have sufficient investment income to cover your expenses and don't need to work from necessity. *This is wealth and financial freedom measured in time.*

If you're free, congratulations and welcome to the freedom club! With this freedom achieved, your focus should be to continue to channel your time and energy to increase your income/expense ratio and net worth through multiple sources of income.

Method 2: The second method is through the money path. Here we take into account your net worth and the equity you have in your investments. If you have assets that don't create a monthly or yearly income but you want to know what your wealth would be as a function of time, you can still do this. Refer to your financial statement and copy across your net worth amount. Divide your net worth by your wealth expenses to ascertain how long your assets would last if you stopped working today. With this method, remember that you will have to liquidate (if you have no savings) some or all of your assets to draw from their equity. You are eating the goose that lays the golden egg, which isn't smart. With Method 1, you protect the goose and live off the eggs.

I hope you now see that financial freedom is much easier than most people think. For too long we've been limited by erroneous information about our financial destiny and freedom. With light now shining, unlock your chains and set yourself and others free.

CHAPTER 10

SIXTY-FIVE/THIRTY-FIVE: THE MAGIC FORMULA

If you know how to spend less than you get, you have the philosopher's stone.
— *Ben Franklin*

Earlier, we discussed the importance of budgets in the wealth journey, and although I don't like to budget, it is necessary, and the process can be made easier if automated. Automation eliminates the need for exercising self-discipline on a consistent basis, and more importantly it places your focus on other areas of the wealth building process such as creating multiple sources of income and increasing your net worth rather than focusing on how to manage what you already have.

There is no universal formula to automation as our personal situations are unique to us and they change with time. You have to determine the strategy that works for you. The key to creating a good system is to make it easy, fun and purposeful. By purposeful I mean that you should keep your ultimate purpose – *financial freedom* – at the core of everything you do. Budgets are usually rejected because the traditional system of budgeting focuses on the negative side of the process and they don't emphasise the positive side enough.

Every future has a price and a promise, but if you focus on the price you have to pay without much regard for the promise (benefits) it becomes difficult to make the necessary sacrifices. The key to the automation system is to make it interesting and exciting by intentionally allowing specific provisions for fun so you can pay the price with ease.

Financial freedom is strongly dependent on how you use the resources you have today, not those you expect in the future. Therefore you need a plan for the distribution of your resources. Below I've detailed a plan that help you reach your financial goal fast and also become financially free. I call this my *65-35 Plan.*

This plan calls for investing 35% of your net income first in yourself (and future) and you living on the remaining 65%. The plan is allocated as follows:

- 10%: tithe/charity investment
- 10%: active investment: (pay yourself first)
- 10%: passive investment (emergency fund, debt elimination fund, and passive investment fund)
- 5%: fun fund (spending money for whatever you want)
- 65%: expenses fund (what you need to live on).

The plan above is only effective if you understand the purpose behind each allocation and with that in mind, I would like to briefly explain each:

Tithe/charitable investment: Generosity is a core part of a rich life, and true wealth (mental, spiritual, physical and material) is incomplete without the art of giving. You have to be willing to give a portion of what you have today (not tomorrow) towards good causes. You make a living by what you earn, but you make a life by what you give. Giving starts the wealth circulation process and opens the door for more to come into your life. (In some cultures and religions, this is encouraged.)

In life, your rewards are usually in proportion to what you give. There is an emotional, mental, spiritual and physical benefit to giving. If you are unable to give away ten per cent, don't let this stop you. Tithing or giving to charitable causes isn't merely about percentages;

rather it is a question of the heart. Ten per cent might seem like a lot but I have found that the joy and peace I have knowing that I can give goes beyond the monetary value of my gift. Start with what you can afford – it's not the amount that counts, it's the habit. You can begin with one per cent and slowly increase the amount; the most important thing is to begin.

I see giving as a duty and responsibility on my part, and I have found that when I give ten per cent away, the ninety per cent remaining seems to meet my needs and more. Giving doesn't guarantee you'll be rich as there are other things you must do. But not giving is a guarantee you will remain poor in spirit as well as unsatisfied with what you have.

Active investment: This is the first step in the wealth creation and multiplication process. You should assign ten per cent of your net income to yourself before anyone else gets paid. This *pay yourself first* principle is an important but often overlooked pathway to financial freedom. One of the wealth philosophies you must adopt is that *a portion of what you make is yours to keep.* Every day you work, you are investing a part of your life in exchange for money, but you must quickly begin to accumulate some of it for yourself so you can reinvest it. Over time you will no longer have to work for money. Instead, your money can start working for you. If you don't pay yourself first, your chances of becoming financially free are slim, but if you can discipline yourself to pay yourself first, you will have what it takes to start your financial freedom journey.

You should invest in your future even if you're in debt. Most people have to wait for three to ten years to get completely out of debt, which is too long to wait to start investing for the future. If your energy is focused on the past alone, you won't have inspiration and hope for the future. You should invest in your future at the same time as trying to rid yourself of all debt. Energy follows focus, and anything that controls your focus controls your life so build your future whilst trying to fix your past.

Ten per cent will get you going on the journey but it won't get you financially free in the fastest time. The truth is that this amount should really be twenty per cent as a minimum if you want to become wealthy within ten years or fewer. I started with ten per cent and I increased my active investment amount soon after – this was one of the shortcuts to attaining my goal. Remember, it isn't the amount that counts, it's the plan. Start with one percent if that is all you can afford and keep increasing it until you're investing the maximum you can without compromising on living properly. The key is consistency, and the best way to do this is to automate it by setting up a system where the money us transferred directly into your investment account as soon as you get paid so you aren't tempted to spend it. Your dream of financial freedom is possible when you start paying yourself first.

Fun fund: This is the part I like the most and where I find that my creativity soars. If you don't include a specific provision for having fun in your planning process, you might find you are unable to sustain your discipline and sacrifice for an extended period of time. Wealth creation is a lifetime process, and one of the reasons you should make fun a priority is so you reward yourself for your hard work. It's important to keep yourself inspired, excited and motivated, and to do this you have to find a way to live normally, and more importantly you need a way to acknowledge your sacrifice and discipline. You don't want to be a like Ebenezer Scrooge from Dickens' *Christmas Carol* who was stingy even towards himself. You need to invest, but you should reward yourself and your five per cent fun fund should be used towards anything you want. Progress creates pleasure, and progress celebrated generates hope and inspiration.

In some sections in this book I make reference to frugality but I don't have in mind the definition that Webster's dictionary gives the word – 'miser' a greedy stingy person who hoards money for its own sake. By 'frugal' I refer to living within your means, saving some of your earnings, and treating your savings as a seed you plant to get a harvest in the future. If you have plenty to spend and live like a pauper, yes, you're a miser and no one should live like a miser. I believe in working hard but also support playing hard. You should have your own method of rewarding yourself, especially if you work, hard, save and invest. Work hard, invest and then you can spend. The challenge today is that with social media and advertising we're encouraged to spend but little is said about investing for the future or the importance of financial freedom.

Passive investment emergency fund: If you've travelled on a commercial flight recently, you will have gone through mandatory safety procedures. The purpose is to ensure that you're safe in the event of an emergency. Similarly, in your life you need to be prepared for any unforeseen financial issues, and this is why you must set aside some money for yourself and your family. Prepare for the worst but hope for the best. You should have at least six months (I prefer twelve months) of your monthly expenses (including liabilities) saved for an emergency before you start actively saving or investing. With your emergency fund securely set aside, you'll be able to maintain your focus on your financial freedom goal, especially in the event of a crisis.

You should create a gulf between your personal account and your emergency account. To do this effectively use another bank account, preferably at a different bank or building society to your usual bank. This is important so you don't see the money. With your emergency fund secure, you can keep your focus on your vision even if you have a temporary setback due to job loss, ill health or another unforeseen situation.

Your emergency fund isn't for saving or investing – it's a security account for your peace of mind. Since this money will hopefully be saved for a long time, you could also save your emergency funds in silver coins or gold rather than a currency which continues to decline in value. Silver and gold are real money. Unlike with a currency, you cannot produce or reprint it and therefore it is more reliable as a protection or insurance plan. Silver is a consumable metal and its value is backed by demand. Both metals have maintained their value in the past decade compared with money and they can be converted back to a currency if needed. Based on today's market conditions and current trends, this might be a good option, but before doing this, study the market trends and seek expert advice.

Your emergency saving plan should be your second priority after your protection plan, and it should precede any investing. Don't delay your emergency saving plan because you have outstanding credit card debt or a loan.

Passive investment debt fund: If you have debts, your passive investment allocation should be directed to your debts after you have securely set side your emergency funds. Most people have to wait for three to ten years to get completely out of debt, which is too long to wait to start investing, but your debts can be reduced if you allocate your passive investment fund appropriately towards your debt fund. Irrespective of the amount of debt you have, you can become debt free by assigning your passive investment amount (ten per cent of your net income) towards your debts. Once your emergency fund is secure and your debts are cleared, you should re-allocate the ten per cent for passive investment towards your active fund so you then have twenty per cent invested towards your better future.

The price

If you can discipline yourself to live within your means by living on sixty-five per cent of your income until you're financially free, you can live the rest of your life the way you want. Most people could reduce the time it would take to become financially free if they decided to stop acting rich. The suggested lifestyle changes will be more bearable for those living below their means compared than those who are living beyond their means. But irrespective of your present lifestyle, it's doable if you believe and are willing to pay the price.

It will be challenging to begin with, but if you persevere it will slowly become simple and painless as the months go on. It's better to make small consistent incremental improvements rather than trying to start big but not continuing after the first few months. If you're living above your means, you should adopt the system immediately but start small. Perhaps you may need to start with a something more suitable to your circumstances – remember it's not the amount that counts, it's the plan.

As you work diligently, there will be changes in your financial life and you will need to manage these carefully – including pay increases. One clever, though challenging, way to get you to financial freedom quicker is to divert salary increases to your active investment. If you find you're managing fine after implementing the 65-35 plan you should divert eighty per cent of any pay increase to your investment account and keep twenty per cent for yourself.

CHAPTER 11

DEAL THE CARDS:
PLAY OFFENCE AND DEFENCE

*Don't tell me what you value, show me your budget,
and I'll tell you what you value.*

— *Joe Biden*

How much do you want to be able to wake up each morning and go to bed at night knowing you're free and have no debts, or if you do they're investment debts that others pay for on your behalf whilst you get richer? If you genuinely have a strong desire for freedom, you need discipline. More importantly, you must become accountable for your personal finances – what, how, where and when your resources are used.

There are two paths to creating the surplus amount required for investing so you can achieve your financial dream of freedom. The first is to earn more. And the best way to do this is to decide on your financial goal or freedom number (per month or year) and add to this amount your expenses (monthly or annually) to obtain the new income you have to earn. This process is called playing offensive and it's the method used by the rich. It's my preference because it focuses on increasing your means rather than living within your means. With this approach you create sufficient allowance for investing without compromising on your lifestyle.

Very few people have been adequately taught about the purpose, function and use of money. And we often lack the essential management skills required to become effective money managers. For most people, it's not an income problem – it's a habit and a lifestyle problem. Your spending will rise to the level of your income unless you remain in control, so it's best to begin with the *defensive strategy* (which involves living within your means) to develop the necessary discipline and skill for wealth.

If you aren't financially free and desire to be, you must spend less than you earn and invest the rest and you can make the process much easier by adopting (temporarily) a budgeting process. A budget makes you accountable, and if you refuse to be accountable, you remove yourself from the path of freedom. Responsibility comes with freedom – you can't have one without the other. Most people think it's too much pressure to follow a budget, but a budget is simply a plan designed to help you achieve your dreams more quickly. Interestingly, those who hate budgets need them the most. The rich and affluent may not have a budget, but anyone who is self-made (including those who started from nothing and created their own wealth) began their journey with a budget, and many still live by the same principles. You start with a budget but you don't stay in one forever. As soon as you've developed the discipline and the habits of being faithful with little things, you can move to the larger and better things by expanding your means.

Unfortunately, my generation is the entitlement generation. We feel that life owes us everything, but we forget life doesn't give us what we want or need; life gives us what we deserve. Before I started budgeting I had the flawed view that it would eliminate fun from my life and I would have to give up the cherished things that gave my life meaning and significance. Not so. Budgeting made me more creative, and creativity makes life exciting and an adventure.

You budget by reducing expenses and increasing income but first you have to start with what you can change immediately – your expenses. Increasing your income (salary, wages) often depends on external factors such as company profits, the economy, clients, customers, or demand/supply of a product or service. You don't have direct control over any of these, but you can control and change yourself. This is where you have to start, especially if you are playing defence. Only a few have really studied and mastered the science of getting rich and can increase their income without relying on external conditions. Therefore, to create changes in your life immediately it is best to begin within – play *defence*.

There are two parts to the budgeting process. The first is the wealth budget, which is a plan to get you financially free within the shortest time by budgeting and investing simultaneously. The second is the secure budget, which is a plan to get you to live within your means first. The secure budgeting path is primarily focused on trying to discipline you to keep your expenses below your income, but it offers no option for saving and investing. The wealth budget will make you wealthy and rich but the secure budget will make you secure and comfortable.

Wealth budgeting

In the wealth budgeting plan you follow the *65-35 Plan;* you invest thirty-five per cent of your net income and live on the remaining sixty-five per cent. With the budget ratio established, your focus should be on reducing your current monthly expenses. This will require creativity and sacrifice on your part, but it's through this process that you begin to develop the habits and lifestyle that will help you become wealthy.

I find that the first thing people say when they hear about the wealth budget is, *I can't live on sixty-five per cent of my income.* In most cases they get upset or launch into a long lecture about why it's impossible. If you feel the same way, I understand, but remember that the quality of the question you ask decides the answer you get. Ask empowering questions from an inquisitive and curious perspective rather than asking disempowering or limiting questions. When you ask disempowering questions you begin to see yourself as a victim rather than victor. Remember that the most important thing is focus, because where your focus goes, energy flows. If you focus on the possibility of making things work, the creative parts of your brain and mind will begin to work to find the right answers. On the other hand, if you think it's impossible, you place limits on your mind.

Let go back to your journal. On a new page, write 'wealth budget'. Next go to the expenses section of the financial statement page in your journal and copy the items from that page. Then follow the steps below:

1) Write down your net income.

2) Calculate what 65% of your net income will be (this is your expenses budget limit).

3) With the baseline set, go through each of your expenses items and identify the items that are wants and needs (separate the wants into essential and luxury).

4) Identify the items that can be reduced or eliminated (permanently or temporarily) to help with your budget process.

5) For the remaining items on your list, go through each and apply the 65% cap to the monthly or yearly expense amount (by multiplying the original amounts copied from your financial statement page by 0.65) to get the new maximum amount you are allowed to spend on that item.

6) Add up your adjusted expenses to get your new estimated total expenses.

7) If your adjusted total expenses is equal to or less than your expenses budget limit, that's good. Otherwise, go through the list again and identify what can be reduced or eliminated. Continue this process until your total recalculated expenses is no greater than your new expenses budget limit.

With your budget set, you are ready to start creating wealth by investing the remaining 35% as directed earlier.

Secure budgeting

In the secure budgeting process, your focus is on getting your overall expenses below your income. This method is primarily for those who are in a deficit each month because they spend more than they earn and cannot follow the 65-35 Plan. Their first priority will be to develop the discipline to live within their means before they can begin to invest. This method won't provide the means for investing because at this stage you are focused on living within your means.

Let's go back to your journal. On a new page, write 'secure budget'. Next, go back to the expenses section of the financial statement page in your journal and copy the items from that page. First, you have to ascertain how to reduce the monthly expenses for each item on your list so what you spend each month doesn't exceed what you earn. The percentage reduction you apply should be based on your income/expense ratio. For example, if your net monthly income is £1,000 and your expenses are £1,200 you overspend by £200 each month and your income-expense ratio is 0.833 (calculated by dividing 1,000 by 1,200) so you'll need to reduce your monthly spend by 16.7%.

Like we did for the wealth budgeting process, go through Steps 1-7 and apply the same principles, but apply the 16.7% correction value to your expenses by multiplying each of the expense items on your list by 0.833 to obtain the new adjusted expense amount. When you reduce your expenses by 16.7% your expenses will be no greater than your income.

As mentioned above, this path leaves you with no room for saving or investing for the future. Reducing your expenses by 16.7 % will get you to ground zero, but to get off the ground so you can start creating wealth, you must increase the percentages. Remember – it's not the amount that counts, it's the plan. Don't focus on where you start, focus on your destination. The secure path budgeting process is the slowest path to financial freedom, but we all have to start somewhere.

With both budgeting methods, you may not be able to apply the correction factor to some of your liabilities because the amounts might be dictated by your creditors, but all debts can be renegotiated and interest rates changed. Don't be quick to dismiss this as possible. Call the companies and see what can be done – get creative. When it isn't possible, some of your unnecessary wants may need to be reduced further or eliminated, or the correction factor increased to make up for liabilities that can't be altered.

Be creative

Below are listed some steps I took to reduce my monthly expenses to give you an idea of things to consider. They might not be applicable to your personal situation but the important thing is to be open to finding possible solutions.

Shop online: By deciding to do my grocery shopping online, I saved £100 on my monthly shopping bills and also I reduced my impulse buying and food wastage by 25%. I also saved two hours each week (104 hours or four days each year) by not travelling to the shops.

Plan in advance: By booking and making reservations in advance, I saved 20% on items such as travelling and other miscellaneous spending. I estimated that I saved £20-40 each month by booking and paying for things in advance.

Shop around: By changing my gym from one in town to another close to home I saved £30. In addition, I saved two hours of travelling each day.

Eating out: I swapped eating out each day for a packed breakfast and lunch at work. This saved me £5 a day (£100 a month) for breakfast and £8 a day (£160 a month) for lunch. In total, I saved £250 each month by opting for home prepared meals.

Negotiate: By negotiating most of my purchases by 20%, I gave myself a 20% income raise.

Delay gratification: By waiting for at least 24 hours before buying anything that wasn't a necessity I reduced my instant gratification purchases. This saved me an average of £100-300 each month on unnecessary clothes and accessories.

Social dining: I reduced my dining in restaurants to once a week. This saved me £200-240 each month.

Alternative bids: I ensured I had 3-4 alternative bids or cost comparisons for all my purchases over £100. There are websites that help you do the work and direct you to the cheapest supplier.

Impulse shopping: I avoided the 'for sale' allure and traps from good advertising. This alone saved me £100-200 each month. I eliminated 80% of my luxury purchases, and for any item I bought, I made sure it was paid for from the income generated by my assets. You want to buy assets and let the income from the assets pay for your liabilities (luxury items).

Applying the tips above (along with a few others) saved me over £1,000 each month. Can you believe it? You'll be amazed at how much you can save if you allow yourself to be creative and are willing to make sacrifices.

The aim of the budgeting process is to reduce your monthly expenses so any surplus money can be channelled into your investment plan or to more important areas in your life. Doing this exercise and reviewing the list each month will not only create more money, it will also highlight your habits. By preparing a budget you gain better accuracy about your current position and the numbers – the numbers are important because they tell a story.

Making it easy

Here is some advice on how to make your budgeting easier:

Think creatively not emotively: The immediate reaction to budgeting is to think with your heart, but let me encourage you to travel up the elevator into your mind and head and think creatively instead. Rather than focus on what you have to give up, focus on what you stand to gain by disciplining yourself for a short time. Most of the sacrifices we have to make in a budget are for things, and there is no joy in things. Joy comes from our relationships and our freedom.

Keep your focus: You may find the budgeting process difficult, especially if you're working on your financial plan as a couple or family because the passion may not be shared at the same level by all parties. If this is true in your case, work as a team and try to keep your focus solely on the shared goal. It's worth it. You really start to live when you're free.

There is no better feeling than choosing to work because you want to rather than because you have to.

Take no prisoners: Anything that stops you or keeps you from becoming financially free is a thief after your promise and destiny – and that includes your desires. You must be uncompromising when pursuing your objectives. Be ruthless towards anything that wants to rob you of your promise. Your mission is financial freedom, complete control of your life, peace and joy. Keep this in mind as you go through this process.

Celebrate taking the island: Find a way to celebrate when you successfully complete your monthly targets. Take some time at the end of each month to admire what you did well, and celebrate by rewarding yourself. You know how much progress you have made when you take time to review your effort. I suggest you find a way to celebrate by making an occasion of the event. Don't just acknowledge yourself – celebrate.

Take massive action: A budget is only a plan and it doesn't guarantee success; the results verify the success or lack therein. Remember, just as it is important to plan your work, you also have to work your plan. Action is king and effort is queen. When you do act, be consistent and persevere.

One reason why some families, couples or teams struggle to be free is because they don't have a shared mission and vision. When people have different philosophies and beliefs about money, the goal of freedom is rarely achieved. Some people believe that the purpose of money is to spend it, others think differently. Many couples fall into this dilemma – one person wants to invest smartly to secure their future but the other wants to spend it all. Both parties have to be in agreement on the vision and should commit to supporting that vision, otherwise it will be much more difficult (not impossible) to achieve financial freedom.

His and hers: If you're a couple or a family, it's a good idea to have individual personal allowances so one party doesn't have to keep asking the other for permission to spend money. You need to include a personal allowance in your budget to cover your individual needs.

All hands on deck: If you're in a committed relationship, married or have a family, you need everyone on board. Mutual respect, trust, sincerity, understanding and – most of all – love is required. Work as a team because the strength of the team is determined by the weakest link. To do this, you need to collectively prepare a mission, vision and purpose statement so there is collective ownership.

Treat it like a business: You must see your financial life as a business, with a vision, mission, and plan. Also, you must see yourselves as executives responsible for making the vision a success. No one should cut corners. There should be a chief executive officer and a chief financial officer – one to protect the vision and the other to manage the finances. One person shouldn't assume all the responsibility while the other does nothing. It's an equal partnership with all parties owning one hundred per cent responsibility for the success of the vision.

Part 4

DON'T NEGLECT IT, OTHERWISE FAILURE LOOMS

CHAPTER 12

THE ULTIMATE SECRET:
CAN YOU MANAGE IT?

At the end of the day we are accountable to ourselves –
our success is a result of what we do.
— *Catherine Pulsifer*

Wealth can only be created, increased, protected, leveraged, and passed on through the principle of effective management. It is perhaps the most important yet least present factor of most people's financial lives, and the reason is that few have been schooled on the importance of management. The word 'management' doesn't usually arouse excitement in us; most people find it boring. It doesn't have a ring to it like 'investing'. In truth, management is the most exciting part of the process if you understand its purpose, especially if you're a good manager. It is important for financial freedom because it's the foundation on which financial fortresses are built.

Effective management is a pre-requisite to wealth protection and multiplication. As mentioned above, wealth isn't created by what you earn, it is created by what you do with what you earn, and I'm surprised by the number of people who dismiss the importance of management. Without management in the wealth equation, failure is inevitable. Any good contractor or engineer will tell you the foundation of a building is the most important part of the structure, although it's rarely visible. The foundation requires engineering and construction skills and attention to detail, not only because it supports the entire building but also because it decides if the building remains standing or is pulled down after construction. If the foundation of a building is condemned due to a major error in construction, the entire building has no further use. Sadly, a lot of people construct their financial futures on weak and defective foundations.

To begin your journey to financial freedom, my recommendation is that you study, practice and make a habit of the management disciplines and principles of wealth before you start acquiring wealth. After graduating with a bachelor's of science degree in engineering, I wanted to become a successful entrepreneur, so I extended my education further by enrolling in a master's degree course in business management. My study and subsequent experience led me to the conclusion that the first thing you should study if you want to be wealthy is not wealth creation but management.

The first problem I notice with people who wish to be financially free is that they see themselves as individuals (a person or a family), and this limits them from seeing the bigger picture. To become wealthy you have to get rid of the idea that you are an individual; you must start seeing yourself as a company (a business). You are the also the chief executive officer (CEO), chief financial officer (CFO), chief information officer (CIO), chief operating officer (COO) of your company. In order words, you are responsible for effectively managing the company's resources to meet its vision and mission.

Businesses (regardless of their type, size or financial position) have basic functions – operations, finance and sales. Therefore, good management of their resources is essential. If you go back to the four roles identified earlier, you will realise these are distinct core areas of a business with specific resources available, and therefore the success of the business hinges on the effective management, delegation and distribution of resources.

80

The reason why few become financially free is due to the mismanagement of resources – rather than allocating their resources efficiently to meet the company's vision, they allow their instant gratification needs to cloud their judgement. In other cases, some have delegated this management responsibility completely to a financial managers or advisors who don't share their vision and have no genuine interest in their success.

The best gift I ever received was hitting rock bottom financially, because it made me understand that the reason I was doing poorly financially was because I was a bad manager. I denied and wrestled with this suggestion for months until I had more than enough evidence in front of me to validate this truth.

To become wealthy, you have to become skilled in managing yourself,
your resources (money, time, energy, effort).

Have you ever wondered why many rich people refuse to give over their entire fortune to their children but instead provide a sufficient amount to ensure they live comfortably while they donate the rest to charitable causes? Some recognise that their children haven't developed their management ability, and they know that anything received too early or too soon without the right support is lost too quickly. Even worse, the individual's life is often ruined. A case in point is lottery winners. Why do people who win millions in the lottery go broke within eighteen to twenty-four months? Lack of management. They haven't developed the character, discipline or wisdom required for that level of responsibility. If you're diligent and faithful in the management of little things, you'll be faithful in large ones – the opposite is also true.

Many of us are trying to manage the large things but haven't mastered the vital few in our personal lives. Wealth is attracted to management. It's created through good management of resources, the organised and efficient use of the available resources to solve problems, and the creation of value for others. Three key points to note from the above statement are *available resources, problem solving, and value creation.* In many homes, resources (income and time) aren't assigned a specific purpose of resolving financial problems. This is evident because most of their problems reoccur on a monthly basis. And this is a result of mismanaging resources.

81

If you were to look closely in your life, how would you score yourself on a scale of 1-10 regarding how you manage your resources (money, time, energy, focus, effort)? Don't be in a hurry to give yourself an 8 or 9 out of 10. You should consider the following questions before you answer:

- Can you describe without referring to a spreadsheet or your bank statement how your income was spent last month?

- Do you know how much you spent on travel, food, groceries, utility bills, social events, eating, clothes and shopping last month?

- Over the past three months what has been the net percentage reduction or increase in your spending in each of the categories in the question above? And why?

- Do you have a financial statement you review and update each month?

- Do you have a management reporting process (statement or similar) you use to keep track of your financial life?

Remember that you are the chief financial officer of your life – these should be part of your responsibilities. You should be answering 'yes' to every question if you are in control of your finances. If you answered 'no' to the questions above, how can you expect life to give you all of the wealth in the world if you can't show you have managed the last thirty days of your financial life effectively?

Many people have little idea where their money goes – all they know is that they don't have enough. Accountability is key, so for the next thirty days write down everything you spend. It sounds like a lot of work but it really isn't. Abbreviate if you need to, but make sure you capture what you spend daily, and at the end of the month add the figures up. This exercise alone will make you more accountable..

Life will not freely give you what you want because you have a desire or passion for it – life gives you what you deserve and (more importantly) what you can manage. And if you can't manage a few hundred or thousand pounds, how could you ever manage a few million pounds? In many cases what you need to do is stop trying to accumulate more and instead focus on adequately managing what you already have, and life will see to it that more comes your way.

Let me illustrate with a personal example of how I allocated my resources at a young age so you can fully appreciate how much I mismanaged my resources.

Monthly expenditure

- Rent: 40%
- Clothes and accessories: 20%
- Social outings: 20%
- Groceries: 10%
- Grooming: 8%
- Personal development: 0%
- Saving and investing: 2%

Daily time usage

- Work (including travel): 10 hours
- Sleep: 8 hours
- TV watching/social media/socialising: 4.5 hours
- Hobbies: 1.5 hours
- Personal development and continuous learning: 0

Can you see the problem? I was a bad manager. The way I used my resources was poor; I was a waster/a consumer rather than a capitalist. I wasn't managing my time or money effectively. I shouldn't have spent 40% of my income on housing – this should have been capped at 30-35%. Even worse, I wasn't investing in myself or for the future and I was spending more on my clothes and accessories than I was spending on my mind (on educating myself). The most important investment is the one you make in yourself. I couldn't save or invest much because I hadn't made investing a priority.

Every time an investor buys a company, the first thing they do is look at the leader and management team to see if they need to be replaced. Why? Money follows management. I was a bad manager and I would have been fired.

Management is about discipline. From my example above, you can see that my habit was to spend all I earned and save what was left, rather than the smarter approach which is to invest first (pay yourself first), then budget and smartly spend. My lack of discipline kept me financially dependent on a pay cheque for years until I began to apply the strategies covered so far in this book in my life. Part of the reason I mentioned earlier that budgeting is essential is simply because it allows you to exercise the principle of effective management. Omit management from your life and you push wealth away from your life.

How well do you manage your resources? You might want to study yourself. Write down your time and money expenditure in your journal and take some time to assign the appropriate monetary and time percentages on how you used your resources in the last three months.

Starting anew

If you come to the conclusion that you have been mismanaging your resources, the first thing to do to create favourable change is to raise your standards. Decide you will develop the skills and knowledge of a competent manager:

Be accountable: Management comes down to this one quality – accountability. You have to take full responsibility for your life, and more importantly you have to be accountable. Like rain –everyone knows they need it, but no one wants to get wet. We find it easy to talk about it but struggle to put our words into action. To become a good manager, your actions have to rise above your excuses.

Be disciplined: The importance of discipline in wealth creation, and protection cannot be over emphasised. You need discipline to manage effectively. If you don't master self-discipline, it will be almost impossible to achieve financial freedom.

Be honest: Honesty is an important quality of a good manager, but most people aren't honest with themselves. Living on credit is living a false life – an illusion. You are living on a salary you haven't earned and that's dishonest. Most people would be financially free more quickly if stopped acting wealthy and start thinking about how they could actually become what they pretend to be. We consume aspirationally, and in anticipation of becoming wealthy, we spend as if we've already have wealth – but we don't. We lead our lives with the hope our dreams will pay off – a big gamble especially with the lifestyles we live. We believe looking the part will get us the dream. If you spend frivolously in anticipation of becoming wealthy, you are unlikely to ever become wealthy. You have to be motivated by your dream to be financially free more than you want to dress, drive, and act and live like you are already wealthy. You must want your goal more than you want or care about the affirmation and opinions of others.

The talents

The ancient story of the parable of the talents is a good way of concluding this chapter on management. According to the story teller, a master was about to travel but, before leaving, he entrusted his resources to three servants according to their abilities. One servant received five talents, the second servant received two talents, and the third servant received one talent. A talent in those days was approximately 50 kilograms of gold and in today's currency each servant was given (in today's currency) approximately £7.5 million, £3 million and £1.5 million which are considerable sums of money. Upon his return after a long absence, the master called in his servants and asked each to give account of the talents he entrusted to them. The first and the second servants explained they'd each put their talents to work (invested) and doubled the value of the talents they were entrusted with, and both were handsomely rewarded. The third servant wasn't a good manager. Rather than investing his resources wisely, he'd buried (saved) his talent in the ground, which meant it produced no return, and he was rebuked, condemned and punished for mismanaging the resources. In addition, the talent assigned to the third servant was taken away and reassigned to the first servant. There is much wisdom to be gained from the story but I want to share ten wealth (management) principles for you to remember:

1) Everyone has been given a gift unique to their abilities and you must effectively manage it by developing and putting it to good use.

2) No one gets the same amount but we all get the same opportunity to put our gifts, talents, skills and resources to good use. Wealth is a not based on what you get but on what you do with what is given to you. You might say 'If I earned more money, I would invest more', but in truth if you managed what you had better, you would have more to invest.

3) Life has expectations of us all. We are expected to multiply and grow in every area of our life, including wealth. Those

who manage what has been assigned to them are compensated handsomely. Those who don't also receive their just rewards.

4) To become wealthy you must become a skilful and intelligent investor. You have to multiply what you receive. Spending all you earn, saving all you earn, and hiding all you earn will not make you wealthy – investing wisely will.

5) Life will evaluate your performance based on what was given to you against your potential to see if you meet or missed the mark. Life never judges you against others – you get judged based on that was given to you and the potential you have within.

6) Your rewards will be in proportion to the price you pay. Wealth is a reward for the sacrifices you make.

7) Life will freely give you what you can manage, and whatever you fail to manage effectively, you will lose.

8) Multiplication is the first rule of money. Money should be invested not saved. If you save, you lose but if your invest and multiply what you have you'll prosper.

9) Money must be protected. Money that doesn't grow, losses its value. Nowadays the servant's talent would have depreciated in value and so he lost some of the money entrusted to him because he failed to protect his capital. In other words, he violated the first rule of investing – *never lose an investment.*

10) Your attitude determines your altitude and outcomes in life. The parable revels the attitude of each servant. Wealth is a matter of attitude, and your attitude in life will determine your outcomes.

CHAPTER 13

CRYSTAL BALL:
YOUR SHORTCUT TO WEALTH

Tell me what you eat, and I will tell you what you are.
— Anthelme Brillat-Savarin

Habits create wealth, not passion, not desire, not even a plan. Your habits make you wealthy or poor. Your life today is a product of your habits of the past, and your future will be shaped by the habits you have today and those you continue to practice. Wealth is a result of or a reward for the actions you take, and actions consistently repeated over time becomes habits. Poverty and wealth are both products of habits – good habits make you rich and bad habits make you poor. No one is destined to be poor or rich. Some are born into affluence and others into poverty, but the key to the futures of all is hidden in the decisions and habits we live by.

Looking back at my childhood and the habits we had as a family I know without a shadow of a doubt it wasn't the economy, the government, the country, the political leaders, other people, or destiny that were responsible for the circumstances and events of our lives. It was the decisions we made daily and the habits we lived by.

One of the cornerstone requirements for financial freedom is the necessity to develop wealth habits. Your habits are important because they decide your character and who you become. And wealth is a function of who you are. To have more, you have to become more, and one of the early questions you should ask yourself in your journey to achieving your financial dreams is: *Who do I have to be first to become financially free'?*

Most people live their lives according to the sequence do-have-be, but this is incorrect. The wealth sequence should be a *be-do-have* model. To have more, you have to do more, but your doing is really a product of who you are. It is less about what you do and more about who you are becoming.

On a piece of paper, make a list of the qualities of someone who is healthy, wealthy and happy – this could also be a list of the qualities you would expect them to have. Write down ten to fifteen items. Next to each quality write down the number 10 – this represents the highest level of excellence in that area. Go through each quality and give yourself a score from a scale of 1-10 on what you believe you are today. It will do you good to be honest with yourself. Do you notice anything interesting about the qualities? They aren't simply wealth qualities; they're qualities that make you a better person.

A number of years ago I tried the exercise on myself. At that time I was single and trying to understand how best to attract my ideal partner into my life. I sat down one evening and asked myself a simple question: *What do I want in an ideal partner?* I started describing my ideal partner in detail, and by the time I had finished I had a huge grin on my face because for the first time I had taken the time to focus my desire towards what I really wanted. I had beautifully painted a portrait of her in words.

Next I asked myself a second question: *What kind of man would she be attracted to and what qualities would he have?* Again, I started making a list of the qualities of this man. Next to each quality I inserted the number 10 to represent how he ranked on the scale. Then I asked myself the tough question: *What score do I give myself on each of the qualities?* I disciplined myself not to be influenced by feedback from my previous relationships. Instead, I challenged myself to be honest and judge myself against the potential I had and how much I'd given. Did I express the highest level of honesty, passion, gentleness, patience, kindness and love? Well, it wasn't a pretty feeling because as I thought deeply, I realised I was living far below who I knew I was. Across twenty qualities, my score averaged between 2-4 .

It dawned on me that life was protecting my ideal partner from me because I wasn't ready to receive her. At that point I would have been a liability to her, not an asset, because I hadn't developed the character I needed for the relationship. I gave myself the assignment of a lifetime – to take my focus away from finding the right partner and instead to focus completely on improving myself and my score to a 9 or 10 in each area. This was life changing to say the least. As I worked on myself, I realised my score increased and I began to attract people who were similar to the portrait of the lady I painted in words. Eureka – I found it. It dawned on me that what you attract into your life is a result of who you are – your character. Success and wealth are what you attract by the person you become.

Each of the qualities I had written down on my list made me a better person in all areas of my life. The true gift to myself from the exercise was that I was making myself a better person, and if it attracted the right woman, fantastic. But if it didn't, it was still fantastic because I was becoming who I was born to be. The destination (becoming financially free) isn't the most important thing; it's who you have to become first that matters.

The ultimate shortcut to becoming the person you want to be lies in your habits, routine and rituals. Your daily habits are like a crystal ball that predicts your future based on your daily actions, feelings and thought. The difference between the wealthy and the poor is simple – wealthy people do consistently what others do occasionally. What you do consistently shapes your life and consistency in action is easier when you identify the daily disciplines and activities that can be turned into habits to be practiced daily. Wealth, financial freedom and prosperity will be in direct proportion to your level of consistency in your application of the daily activities and actions needed for wealth.

Consistency is why some people become wealthy, while others remain average. Usually, it has nothing to do with gender, IQ, age, ambition, or desire but has everything to do with being deliberately consistent. Consistency in daily routines and habits separates billionaires from millionaires, the wealthy from the poor, top-level athletes from amateurs, CEOs of large corporations from employees, and happily married couples from other couples.

To develop the right wealth habits you need practice and repetition, and the best way to make this habitual is to discipline yourself for one hundred days without exception. If you do this, the habit will become automatic and instinctive. The reverse applies for ridding yourself of an unwanted habit.

The lifestyle

Those who are rich, wealthy and happy live in a certain way. Their choice of lifestyle provides the environment for them to create more, successfully protect, multiply and share their wealth. Most people feel the sacrifice and discipline required for becoming financially free restrictive, and because of this they refuse to adopt the lifestyle of the wealthy. There are four lifestyle choices that will help you achieve financial freedom:

Low maintenance: People often confuse the term 'low maintenance' with 'cheap' or 'frugal' but that isn't what I mean. Anything that requires high and regular (unnecessary) investment of your time, energy, effort, money and thought should be avoided or replaced so you can live a pleasurable lifestyle. Doing this will reduce your worry, fear, and unruly thoughts. You will also focus your thoughts on things that are noble, pure, just, sincere, beautiful but more importantly things that can help you increase your wealth. Maintenance diminishes joy.

There's a difference between looking wealthy and being wealthy. Most people who look wealthy aren't actually wealthy – they live above their means and have low cash reserves. Interestingly, some of those who don't look wealthy are wealthy and have a surplus of reserves. I didn't inherit a wasteful lifestyle – there was little to waste, and I think that in some way that helped me to avoid much of the consumer lifestyle. If you're born poor, you often hold unto some of your poor habits, and in some part my early low maintenance lifestyle helped me achieve financial freedom. We wasted little, because we had little. The hyper-consumption lifestyle wasn't something I experienced, so a lot of my lifestyle decisions today are easy to make. I don't act rich or wealthy because I know I'm not what I wear, I'm not where I live, and I'm not even what people say I am. Having a low maintenance lifestyle creates freedom – those who have one aren't controlled in their emotions, mind or materially by the things they own. The amount of time, energy, effort (mental and physical) exerted by a few people on things that don't add any meaningful contribution to their lives would surprise you. Whatever controls your focus controls your life. The wealthy understand this and they choose a low maintenance lifestyle.

Delayed gratification: If you can control yourself and delay gratification, you already have the qualities to make you wealthy. Instant gratification is one of the major reasons why most people fail to achieve financial freedom. Our fascination and obsession with consumption) and the need to have it all immediately, in many cases using personal debt, is one reason why many remain financially dependent and servants to money. Delayed gratification is one of the success traits you need to become wealthy. People who delay gratification are generally more stable and successful. Delayed gratification is a decision, a habit and a lifestyle. It will help you achieve your financial dreams more quickly.

Neighbourhood: For some people, their place of residence is often influenced by what others will think of them and of the area. To fit in we try to look the part, drive and dress to suit the expectations of others and our environment. Nothing has a greater impact on your wealth and consumption than your choice of home and neighbourhood. If you aren't already wealthy and live in a pricey home in an expensive or affluent neighbourhood, you will spend more than you should and your ability to save and build wealth will be compromised.

We tend to act and behave like those in our social circle, and as a result those who live in some neighbourhoods will often try to fit in or compete with those around them. Where you live (whether you own or rent) is the biggest deterrent to your financial freedom, and it's much harder to live below your means in a high occupational status, hyper-consuming neighbourhood, primarily due to influence by association. When you choose a neighbourhood, you also choose a lifestyle. The house you live in should not and does not define you:

Warren Buffet, the second richest man in the world, still lives in the house he bought in 1958 for $31,500.

Continuous learning: Continuous learning is integral to the lifestyles of the rich and wealthy. Wealth is a product of who you are (your character), but your character depends on your investment in yourself. Financial wealth is heavily dependent on the acquisition of knowledge, understanding, and the application of the knowledge based on sound judgement. You have to invest in yourself because your value increases in proportion to your wisdom. The wiser you are, the more you can see opportunities, identify problems to solve, create value for people, and become wealthy. If you wish to be and remain successful, invest a minimum of five to ten per cent of your income each month and your time each day on your personal growth and development. The wiser you become, the easier it will be to achieve freedom. Just like you feed and nourish your body daily, you have to do the same for your mind by continuously feeding and developing it for mental and emotional stamina and wellbeing.

Frugality: Most people hate this word. Frugality isn't about deprivation or being cheap. It's about making your money go somewhere that matters more rather than somewhere that matters less. What some consider an inconvenience, I consider to be a privilege. You might attribute that to my poor upbringing, and maybe you're right, but I don't consider this something to be ashamed of. It earned me my freedom. To become wealthy, especially if you start from the bottom, you have to learn to avoid the all-consuming lifestyle of keeping up with the Joneses. This by far is the hardest discipline to master. If you're worried about how others will perceive you OR if you allow your decisions and feeling to be based on the opinions of others, you'll never be free. You might become wealthy, but true freedom will elude you.

CHAPTER 14

FIRST CURRENCY: INVEST IT WISELY

Every day is a bank account, and time is our currency. No one is rich, no one is poor, we've got twenty-four hours each.

— *Christopher Rice*

One of the key distinctions between the rich and poor is hidden in how both use time, even more in how they value time. Success requires investing time in significant activities that provide the highest return in the future, and the effective use of time is the best-kept secret of the highly successful and the wealthy. It's truly rare to meet a wealthy and successful person who doesn't value their time highly. Conversely, it's rare to find an average and unsuccessful person who values time. Time is the raw material for wealth creation, and we all receive equally the same amount each day for the primary purpose of investing it wisely towards any experience we want from life.

The key to your wealth is to treat time and money as if they're the same. Like money, your time has to be used resourcefully. Wealth creation begins with the understanding, application, and wise investment of time. Bypass this process and you don't stand a chance of financial freedom. Financial wealth is a product of what you have, what you have is a function of what you do, what you do is a result of who you are, but who you are (or will become) depends on how you invest your time.

The way you use your time is the crystal ball to your future. If you studied or observed your time usage over a seven day period, you could predict the likelihood of your becoming wealthy. This is because the way you use your time identifies your priorities. Every day you get twenty-four new hours, and how you use each hour decides who you become and what you have. Time is the only thing we are given in equal quantity and proportion. We have varying levels of talent, intellect, drive and passion. But each of us is given exactly twenty-four hours a day – no one gets more. The fundamental thing that sets the wealthy and rich apart from the rest is how they use their twenty-four hours.

I used to say, 'I wish I had more time'. The problem with this statement is that it highlights an attitude of ignorance, because no matter how much you want more time, you can't get it. It's impossible, and to wish for it is naive. A better question to ask is 'How can I intelligently use my time?' Lousy questions attract lousy answers, and likewise the right questions attract the right answers.

How we use our spare time is often the reason our financial dreams elude us. Wealthy and rich people use time differently; they understand that true wealth is created by the appropriate allocation of their time and they spend time with their families and friends and invest the rest wisely in increasing their financial intelligence and looking for opportunities to increase their wealth.

When I worked as an employee, I knew I couldn't get wealthy during my working hours by exchanging my time for money but I also knew I could slowly build my way to wealth on a part time basis if I reversed the role and got money to work for me. Every day I dedicated a few hours of my personal time to study, learning, analysing and taking small steps towards my financial dreams and goals. Financial wealth can be created part time – you can start where you are with whatever time you have – but the key is to do it daily and consistently. The first thing people say to me is, *You don't know what my day is like.* If you want excuses, your mind will find a thousand reasons for you, and when you're done using them up, it will generate another thousand. Drop the 'lack of time' excuse and instead get creative so you can see how your day can be restructured to allow you enough time to build your financial dreams. To begin, let us analyse a typical day and see how you can find some time.

Each day is split into two distinct parts – your waking day and night (your sleep time). The average working adult uses their time as follows:

- Sleep: 6-8 hours
- Work: 8 hours
- Pre and post work activities (includes preparation for work and travel to and from work): 4 hours
- Spare time (personal): 4-6 hours

For most people their spare time during the working week is often four hours a day (typically from 7 pm to 11 pm, assuming standard working hours), and how you use this time is really the key to your success or lack of it. Some people use up much of this time on social media and entertainment. There's nothing wrong with either but the time invested should be proportionate to your dreams and the future you wish to create. Did you know that the average person spend four to six hours daily on social media or watching TV? This is why most people remain poor. If you really want to become wealthy, you have to discipline yourself to invest a minimum of one or two hours every day towards your personal development and growth to help you create a better future.

The average person can afford to maintain their current lifestyle and still invest some time in increasing their wisdom and financial intelligence. By carefully planning and managing your time each day it's possible to allocate some time towards your continuous learning without using any of your spare time. There are two simple methods I used without making drastic changes to my lifestyle:

Tip 1: Wake up one hour earlier each day and invest the first hour in yourself. You might say 'I must have eight hours of sleep to function properly' and that's acceptable if you're already wealthy. If you aren't and are healthy (with no medical conditions), you haven't earned the right to be in bed for eight hours each day. Remember, this is a book on creating wealth and achieving financial freedom, so before you get emotional, please answer the question: *Is your desired future worth investing one hour of your sleep time each day?* If your answer is no you might want to give this book to someone who has bigger dreams. One hour each day is equal to one day each month or fifteen days each year, which (if invested wisely) will significantly increase your likelihood of becoming wealthy.

Let's consider an alternative. If we assume that for some personal reason, you can't invest one hour of your sleep time towards your future, that's not the end of the world because there is another way.

Tip 2: Combine your travel and leisure time with learning. The average person spends approximately two hours travelling to and from work and one or two hours on recreational activities like running or going to the gym daily. By combining your travel and leisure or downtime with your learning time, you can invest sixty minutes each day in your personal development and growth. This can be done by reading a book or listening to an audiobook, a podcast, or an educational audio recording on your mobile device when travelling or exercising.

If you invest one hour each day in reading one book to increase your financial intelligence, you can read two books each month. In a year you would read twenty-four books. In five to ten years you could become knowledgeable in the area of financial wealth and be an expert on wealth. Your life would never be the same if you resolve to invest one hour each day towards reading. The question isn't Can you?; it's Will you?' If your goal for financial freedom is an absolute must, you will do whatever it takes. If it isn't, you will come up with an excuse, like many do.

Your time's value

The value of something is not only decided by the price you are willing to pay for it. It's also influenced by its rarity. The reason the Oppenheimer Blue diamond was sold almost for £40 million at Christie's auction house in Geneva in 2016 was because blue diamonds are exceptionally rare (comprising around 0.0001% of the world's diamonds) and also because someone perceived it to be of greater value than the price set by the seller. Rarity increases value but not always, what often counts is what others are willing to give in exchange for what you have. Once you start to invest your time in increasing your wisdom, you start to increase your value. Time is rare – you can't buy, store, save, manage or control it. You can only use it as it comes each day. Although time is rare, the perceived value of your time is based on what others are willing to pay for it. You control the value of your time because you decide the problems you solve and (more importantly) the value you create for others.

Money is a measure of the reward you receive for the value you create for others. The more valuable your time becomes, the more you can increase your wealth. To become wealthy you have to constantly increase your time's value. To do this you have to become more valuable, and this can be achieved in many ways.

Working the numbers

Clarity combined with specificity is how dreams are fulfilled; you need to know exactly what you want. First, decide how much you want to be worth (in time) or how much you want to earn, then add to this amount your expenses and this will give you your new desired annual income.

Financial goal (FG) + annual expenses (AE) = desired annual income (DAI).

Once you know your desired annual income, your time (the raw material for all wealth) has to be utilised so the value increases to the same or a greater amount than your desired income. There are fifty-two weeks in a year (for simplicity I'll assume there are fifty working weeks with two weeks allocated for holidays). With forty working hours in a week, you have 2,000 working hours a year. Let's assume you currently earn

£25,000 each year but you would like to earn £1 million. At £25,000, the value of your time is £12.50 an hour. To make a million a year, you have to earn £500 an hour. Although you don't currently earn £500 an hour, you have to start using your time as though it were worth that much. By adopting this philosophy, the way you think will begin to change radically and you will find that as your thoughts change, your actions, habits and behaviour will also change and consequently your results. By choosing your desired time's worth you will begin to notice changes in your life. When you are undertaking a task you ask yourself: *Is what I'm doing worth £500 an hour?*

This is the philosophy you should adopt if you wish to be wealthy. By focusing on ways to increase your value you will start to see and attract the right opportunities. Each time you invest an hour you should ask yourself empowering questions such as: *How can I get £500 worth of value from each hour?* As you read the remaining chapters of this book you should be looking for something worth £500 in value for each hour invested. This new attitude will do two things for you – it will make you more conscious of how you use your time and how you can increase the value of your time. And more importantly it will make you more creative; you will suddenly become a treasure hunter looking for the hidden jewel in every experience. As you can imagine, you won't be able do this in all areas of your life, so you must become strict with what and how you spend your time. You will have to discipline yourself to stop doing things that are worth less than £500 an hour. This can be achieved easily by adopted the leverage principle, especially in your personal life. By using other people's time, energy and experience you can delegate most of your routine tasks, including all activities that others can do equally or better than you, such as your grocery shopping, domestic chores like cleaning or other low wage activities. This will allow you to invest the leveraged time to wealth building strategies. Your goal may not be and does not have to be £500 an hour. I have only used this as an example and you can choose any figure you want. It doesn't matter what you earn now. If you hold onto your vision and emotionalise it with feelings and desire you will start to act like the person you see in your vision – self-image decides performance. For this to be effective you must first change you image of yourself in your subconscious mind about yourself. See, feel, believe and begin to act like the person you want to become and your world will change before your eyes.

Part 5

MAKING THE MOST IMPORTANT
DECISION

CHAPTER 15

MY STORY:
WHAT'S THE PRICE
OF YOUR DREAM?

It is not in the stars to hold our destiny but in ourselves.
— *William Shakespeare*

That I am free today is not down to luck, faith, or good fortune. Rather, it's a result of my willingness to follow a carefully tailored plan and execute my strategy vigorously. If I had to pinpoint where the breakthrough moment occurred, I would say it was the day I decided to raise my standards. That might sound too simple, but my decisions, actions and life changed when I decided financial freedom was an absolute must. I had arrived at a place in life where I was tired of being average; I had a family who looked up to me for leadership, support, direction and hope, and I had to be the pillar of support they needed. If you find your why, the 'what' and 'how' become much easier. All the 'how to's' will serve no purpose until you have your 'why'. Your why is the fuel that gets you off the launch pad and keeps you travelling in the direction of your dreams. How is it possible that I arrived in London from Nigeria as a student with no money, no friends, and no family or support around me and eight years after arriving, I was financially free? *I had a dream I was willing to die for, not live for.*

Until you find that thing you are willing to give everything you have for, you might never see your dreams become a reality. The best advice I can give you is to find your compelling reason for wanting freedom, because until you have it and until you decide you are not willing to live in any other future but the one you want, you might fall short of the mark.

Was it easy? Absolutely not but what does easy or hard have to do with anything? If it were easy, everyone would be rich and happy. You simply need to have the mindset that you will get it done – easy or hard. When I decided to leave my country of birth in pursuit of a better life, I knew it would be tough but I was willing to do it hard.

You can have the biggest dream, but between your dream and its achievement are a number of critical and necessary steps. Your dream must be converted to a goal, given a timeline, converted into a master plan and developed into a strategy, and finally formulated into habits which you must execute daily through discipline, sacrifice, hard work, consistency and patience before it can ever become reality. Until you are willing to go through each stage of the process, your dreams might elude you.

Give yourself permission

In 2008, I had nothing. I was in debt and the income I earned was far less than my monthly expenses leaving me with more days left at the end of each month than I had money. Despite my financial position, I decided to set myself a goal of becoming financially free within ten years. At this point in my life it seemed farfetched, but I was willing to give myself the permission to dream, and that is how achievements are realised. You simply need to give yourself permission to dream, to choose and to decide. It isn't what you don't have that is stopping you from leading the life you deserve; it is often the resources you think you need. My experiences have taught me that if you can decide what you want and act with expectation, everything is set in motion and life will start to bring towards you the resources and opportunities you need to help you make your dreams a reality.

I started with a dream, then it became a goal. But it became reality because I made, and worked my plan. My strategy included three years of study during which time I bathed my mind, brain and heart with the wealthy strategies of successful people followed by a five year continuous process of modelling their beliefs, habits, behaviour and lifestyle. It was that simple. I followed my plan and by December 2014 I achieved my dream; I was financially free and I retired from my engineering profession eighteen months afterwards.

Whatever it takes

What are you willing to sacrifice for freedom? There is a common misunderstanding that anyone can achieve any goal without exchanging or sacrificing something in return. To become wealthy, sacrifice is a must: you have to change the way you think, the associations you keep, and yourself. I had to do the same, and it was worth it. There are four things you have to change:

Thoughts: Wealth is a product of your thoughts. You have to change the way you think because your thoughts decide your destiny. Changing your thoughts begins by changing what you see and hear, the influences around you and the questions you ask yourself. At the early stage of my journey, I didn't have direct access to the mentors I admired but I had access to their thoughts – in written and spoken words – so I spent a lot of time reading, studying and listening to books, audio and video material containing the best wealth ideas, principles and strategies. I also read a lot of biographies and autobiographies because it was equally important to understand the person behind the words. I had to change my thoughts from the poverty stricken mindset I grew up in to one of abundance, affluence and prosperity, and I could only achieve this by displacing my old pattern of thinking with success beliefs. Everything begins at thought level, so to change your life you must first change your thoughts.

Friends: One of the benefits of setting goals and having dreams is because it helps you choose your associations and filters your inner circle of mentors, friends, and peer groups. All your relationships will affect you; there's no such thing as a neutral relationship – some will pull you down and others lift you up. To achieve your financial dreams, you need to be surrounded by like-minded people, quality people who can help you become all you can be. As the Bible says, '*Iron sharpens iron*, so one man sharpens another.' If you walk with the wise you will become wise, and the opposite is also true. You will find that as you grow and invest in yourself, you will outgrow some friends who are not intentional about their personal growth and development. The changes in your life will demand that you walk away or spend less time with some people. Some friends will also walk away from you because they don't feel comfortable with your dreams and the changes they see in you. The vacuum created will help you find the right associations and relationships you need for the future you want.

Mentors: In the wealth journey there are two ways of achieving your dreams – through your experiences alone (often mistakes) or by combining your experiences with other successful people's experiences (mentors). Mentors provide a shortcut to success, and who you learn from writes your future. Mentors expand you, and your ability to learn from them will give you the best chance of becoming wealthy and successful. The shortcut to wealth is to develop a strong thirst for positive associations and learning from others, because the right people can take you further than you can go on your own. Your ability to listen, learn, and follow the advice of good mentors, and accept their corrections, will speed you towards financial freedom. You attract into your life whatever you admire. If you admire the wealthy and rich, you will be attracted to them and you will be open to learning from them. If you resent them, you'll reject their wisdom and unfortunately never be one of them. An important question to ask yourself is 'Who is my financial hero or mentor and what has been the proof that my learning from them is creating the desired results?' My financial freedom is a gift from the mentors who have poured wisdom into my life through their experiences and teachings. I was taught well by the best, but more importantly I was open to their advice. Your life isn't a product of what you were taught or what you learned; your life is a product of your beliefs. Learning alone does nothing, unless you believe and are willing to act on your conviction. Your financial future depends on who's mentoring you and the philosophies you adopt. I chose to believe and, as they say, the rest is history

Old self: Financial freedom requires the sacrifice of who you are today for who you need to be in the future. Just like a caterpillar has to die to give birth to its new self – a butterfly – you too have to let go of specific parts of your old lifestyle to adopt the habits, character, lifestyle required for wealth. I'm not the same person I was as a teenager; I changed, and I don't mean just physically. I let go of parts off my old self to make way for the person I am today. I often hear the words *You have changed* when I meet old acquaintances and friends, and each time I smile silently because it means I am growing and progressing towards my potential. The longer you hold to your past, the more you sacrifice your true destiny. Many people hold onto an old identity and image of who they once were and refuse to become their best self – as though they have some form of allegiance to their past. If you're not financially free, why not be open to trying things differently? This doesn't mean you have to become someone completely different. You simply have to be willing to let go of the good for the best and the best for the great.

OK, let's begin

In developing your plan, you have to start with the numbers. First you should identify your basic financial needs and separate them from your desires or wants – you did this earlier. Your basic needs (food, water, shelter, rest, security and safety) are different to your self-esteem (status, dominance) and self-fulfilment needs (realising personal potential, self-fulfilment, seeking personal growth and peak experiences). The amount required for your basic needs (including some selected wants/desires) is much smaller than most people think. The important thing to remember is that financial freedom is achieved when your financial needs are met without you having to work unless you choose to. It's achieved more quickly if you begin with your basic needs (expenses) and expand your expenses amount to include your wants and desires. If you start with your desires and a luxury lifestyle, you might find that the monetary amount stops you from starting your journey. This is one of the major reasons why many are still financially dependent. Lifestyle changes are often necessary to begin the journey, and those willing to make the necessary changes are those who succeed quickly. Your strategy should be to become financially free based on the basic necessities you need to live a comfortable lifestyle. Once you're financially free, you can increase your means and your expenses to accommodate other wants and desires (prestige and luxury needs).

Working the numbers

Step 1: Identify what you need. To begin you need clarity regarding what your necessary expenses are each month – this should be an easy exercise as you have most of the information from your financial statement. My first step was to identify and itemise my monthly expenses so I could review and reprioritise my spending habits. To be financially free I needed to have an investment income stream capable of generating the same or more than my monthly expenses. At that time I had a job that funded my lifestyle, but my goal was to get to a place where I could maintain my lifestyle without having to work because it was a necessity. I had no investments, but I knew that to live off the income from investments, I had to adjust my spending habits so I could save, invest and start building my own wealth. I was clear about my priorities and it wasn't difficult for me make the necessary sacrifices required to reduce my monthly expenses. By identifying my basic necessities and most important wants I was able to go through my expenses and eliminate the unnecessary (though nice) things I spent money on each month.

This exercise reduced my expenses drastically. I was left with a monthly expenses budget of £2,500 and could live on this each month and still maintain a good lifestyle. This allowed me to divert all surplus towards my investment fund and made the goal of becoming financially free more realistic.

Step 2: Ascertain your passive income goal. With my new monthly expenses of £2,500 established, I needed passive income created from investment greater than this amount. In addition, the passive income had to be consistent and continuous and not require much of my time (except for the occasional time spent in management). I figured that if I could do this, I would be financially free because (except for unforeseen circumstances) my income would cover my expenses.

You don't need to have a million pounds in your bank account to be financially free. Freedom is cheaper than you might think. It's not dependent on a magic number; it depends on you – your lifestyle – and it comes when you have a reliable and steady source of investment income (that doesn't require you to work) which exceeds your expenses. And this amount is much lower than most people think. Begin with your basic needs (and most essential wants), and once you're on Freedom Island, you can start expanding your means and adding more desires, wants and necessities. Many millionaires are not free and many free people are not millionaires. Your lifestyle decides when and if you become financially free.

Step 3: Choose your investment path. After completing Steps 1 and 2 above, I was clear about the new lifestyle I had to adopt, and I knew the level of income I had to generate. The next step was to secure the investment that would create the passive income I needed, but I knew nothing about investing, so I chose an investment path to study. I continued to work as engineer but during my spare time I was working on becoming an investor.

Step 4: Take action. After I'd studied and invested in my financial intelligence for a few years, I was ready. Planning is great but when the time for action comes, take action. I chose three paths to wealth – business, property and building a personal brand – and I started with property. For anyone starting their wealth journey, property investment is the quickest path to financial freedom; no investment can get you quicker to your financial dreams if you understand the game. It has always offered the best returns for the least risks. But it requires strong financial education and intelligence, so my recommendation is for you to invest in financial education first – don't accept anyone's opinion about investing. I started with property because I had no money and I knew it offered the opportunity to safely use debt leverage to achieve my goals through other people's money.

Single point of failure

In engineering, we often talk about a 'single point of failure' for systems. Depending on the nature of the business operation the system serves, it's often important to design in sufficient redundancy (back up provision) on some of the systems. This ensures that in the event of a catastrophic or unforeseen failure of the system, there' is sufficient back provision to maintain the business critical systems, thus avoiding major losses – both tangible and intangible.

You probably understand the logic behind this, so my questions are: Do you have a single point of failure in your financial life? What happens if you can't work? What would happen to your family if you died suddenly? What would happen if you were fired or the company you work for closed down? I don't wish any of these to happen to you, but things *do* happen and it's better to be prepared. We understand the importance of continuity in business and system design but we don't grasp the fact that our lives and families are more important and also need some level of redundancy.

One reason I made the necessary sacrifices was because I understood the implications of having a single point of failure, and I had one – *a job*. There's nothing wrong with having a job but it offers you no security and no leverage – you have to work to earn and it's a single point of failure if you have no other income streams. If you have only one income stream, one of the important components of your freedom plan should be to start building multiple sources of income. To do this effectively, you will have to endure temporary inconveniences for a short period so you can live the rest of your life the way you want. The adjustments needed in your lifestyle, and the discipline required to place you in a position where you can start investing in your future, will require changes. You might be tempted by the emptiness of delayed gratification because of what others think or say, but you shouldn't care too much about what others think – it's your life, after all. Many lives are hugely influenced by the opinions of people, and also many destinies remain unfulfilled because of the lack of courage required to live without conforming to the expectations and standards of others. Until you stop focusing on living your life according to other people's standards and start living your life on your own terms, you will never be free.

My first move

My first investment was a two-bedroom property in London. It cost £215,000 but I was able to obtain a mortgage of £185,000 and pay a deposit of £30,000 which took me two to three years to save. Prior to choosing property, I did some due diligence on various investment options and discovered that no other investment product offered the same or a similar level of leverage. I only would have been entitled to an investment of the same amount had I chosen paper asserts (stocks, bonds), gold, oil or other investments worth £30,000. I chose property because, although I had only £30,000 to invest, the bank was willing to loan me 85% of the money I needed for an investment seven times my equity.

I'm not recommending you follow the same path for the simple reason that debt is risky and it requires a lot of financial intelligence. You shouldn't use debt leverage unless you have sound financial knowledge, understanding and wisdom. Before getting into property investing I spent two to three hours daily for three years on my financial education. I studied the strategies used by my mentors, and today I still invest a few hours daily on my financial education. Property investing is finance and management intensive; you need education and experience in both, and it's simple, but not easy. You have to invest in your financial intelligence heavily before using debt, and more importantly you have to become a brilliant analyst. To purchase a single property, I had to analyse one hundred properties. I shortlisted ten and from the ten I made an offer on three before selecting one. This is called the *100-10-3-1* rule which I learned from my mentors. It's so important that I'll repeat it again. Before purchasing a property, you should study, analyse and complete the due diligence (and write up) on one hundred properties, then shortlist ten for further analysis. Make an offer on three and purchase one.

Now what?

After my first investment, I needed to increase my financial IQ if I was going to buy more, so I went back to the drawing board – to study, to learn and prepare. Two years after my first investment, I was ready for my next, so I refinanced my first investment and pulled the initial equity from it to use as a down payment for my new investment. Even after refinancing, my income from the first investment still exceeded my expenses, and with none of my capital in the investment I have an infinite return on my investment. In addition to getting my money back, my estimated net worth had increased by over £250,000 because the property's value had increased from £215,000 to £470,000.

Next, I found another property and, with my original capital from my first investment combined with the money I had saved, I purchased another investment. This also produced a positive cash flow and again I went back to the drawing board, This time I only waited for a year to refinance. This is the secret to property investing – it is called the *velocity path* to wealth. You don't park your money in an investment for too long; you put some overalls on it and keep it moving. The quicker the speed, the richer it makes you.

By carefully using debt leverage to invest, I arrived at a point where the income I was generating was sufficient to cover my expenses. At that point, I was out of the rat race, and with my new found freedom I channelled my focus on creating multiple income streams to generate income every month.

This book you are reading is one of my passive income streams; I receive an income through royalties for each sold. The key is to create passive income streams that feed each other. The income stream from one investment should support another where possible. With my property portfolio foundation in place and growing, and other passive income streams secured, I moved to the second phase of my plan which was building a business and developing a personal brand.

Investing through a business is where wealth is multiplied through the wealth strategies used by the rich – debt and taxes. Both strategies are advantageous to entrepreneurs, business owners and investors rather than employees. Taxes are the single largest expense for employees, with up to 50% of their gross income spent in one or more categories – *income, national insurance, consumption or value added tax (VAT), excise duties, motor tax, stamp duty and inheritance tax.* In the case of an individual, the government gets paid first but with a business, the government is paid last. This means that businesses can create wealth, pay all business expenses, and re-invest before paying any taxes on their profits. This significant incentive creates a huge advantage, especially when other tax incentives available to businesses are factored in. When combined with the debt leverage opportunities available to business owners and investors, it creates an unfair advantage, and for this reason the rich get richer. If you want to be wealthy, you should aspire to become a business owner and/or an investor instead of remaining as an employee so you can benefit from the same advantages. You must get money to start working for you as soon as you can.

Currently my property and paper asset investments keep me financially free, but my business will make me rich. I explain this because you need to know the purpose of each investment vehicle so you can choose the right plan and path for you. Had I started with any other investment vehicle, I might not be financially free today, but because I started with property it provided me with the opportunity to use leverage (other people's money) to achieve my dreams.

A silver lining

One reason I'm financially free today is because I was born and grew up with little; I wasn't spoilt and I didn't grow up with a sense of entitlement. My parents couldn't afford everything I wanted and so most of the things that make people feel secure or significant rarely excited me, and this made delaying gratification easier.

Security has never been attractive to me because I didn't grow up with the fear of losing anything – you can't lose what you never had. Today I'm comfortable with and in life because I know that if lose all I own, I will be returning back to a place I know how to handle. More importantly, I have developed the habits and character I need to attract wealth back into my life. This eliminates fear from my life, and therefore I'm free – mentally, emotionally, spiritually and also materially.

I'm financially free today and if I can do it, you can.

CHAPTER 16

CHOOSING YOUR VEHICLE: INVEST LIKE THE RICH

If you do not change direction you may end up where you are heading.
— Lao Tzu

To travel from London to Paris, you can travel via various means – you can fly, travel by train, drive, cycle or travel by foot. It will take approximately 1 hour 20 mins to fly, 6 hours if you drive, 2.5 hours via the Eurostar, 23 hours if you cycle, and 58 hours if you walk. Each choice will get you to your destination, so technically you achieve your goal, but you have to look beyond the outcomes. The model taught for years is to get a salaried job and work for forty years and retire financially secure at sixty-five so you can live out the reminder of your life. This is not only an obsolete idea, it's also the worst vehicle for your journey to financial freedom because it requires the direct exchange of your time, energy, effort, focus, wisdom and presence. There are essentially two routes to wealth – people (using time) working to acquire wealth and money (in the form of using leveraged resources) working to acquire wealth. The former relies on a single source to create wealth and the latter relies on multiple sources to create wealth.

There is a wide variety of wealth vehicles available today, many more than were available fifty years ago. The vehicle you choose is important but it isn't as important as the plan supporting that vehicle. In choosing the right vehicle and route, there are four questions to ask:

1) How long will the journey last? In other words, how quickly can you get there?

2) Upon arrival will you be able to enjoy the wealth you created? It's one thing to be wealthy; it's another to be wealthy and healthy. Many achieve the former, few attain both.

3) Who will you become en route to the destination? This is by far one of the most important factors in the whole process. Using professional managers to help you create wealth is OK, but if it robs you of the opportunity to increase your financial IQ, you should rethink your approach.

4) What state will you be in on arrival? We tend to exchange our health to get wealth, and once we've achieved wealth we spend it to buy health.

Your choice of vehicle should take the leverage principle into consideration. Based on the London-Paris travel options identified earlier, you would probably agree with me that flying or using the train is the best option because of the power of leverage – doing more with less. All other options require physical labour; they take much longer, more effort and energy, and offer little or no leverage. The problem is that many people are trying to get wealthy through the most physically demanding vehicle and route.

To achieve wealth you should focus more on money (in the form of using leveraged resources) working to acquire wealth. There are numerous vehicles for creating wealth using this route of which the main ones are businesses, property, commodities and paper assets. Each has its unique advantages but the ultimate advantage lies between the investor's two ears – what you know. One of the first rules of wealth creation is that you should invest in yourself first.

Secondly, you should invest in what interests you, attracts your passion or is something you want to know a lot about. Otherwise, you won't manage it well or persevere when the going gets tough. Many people invest in stocks, bonds, commodities or property but fail to invest in increasing their financial intelligence. They fail to see that the key to remaining financially secure depends on their financial IQ. Property, gold or paper assets don't make you wealthy. It's what you know about each investment vehicle and how you apply that knowledge that makes and keeps you wealthy. Your financial wisdom is the key.

Financial wealth begins with education, and your decision to invest continuously and commit to the discipline of constant never ending improvement in your financial education will decide the longevity of your wealth. You are fully responsible for your financial future, so don't rely completely on experts. Wealth creation isn't a passive strategy; it's an active strategy that requires the investment of your time.

The magic in part time

I started part time. If you weren't born wealthy and didn't fall on good fortune, you too will have to begin part time. When I began my journey, I had a full time job, together with other personal responsibilities, and the time I had available was limited. I decided to start my journey on a part time basis by investing some of my spare time each day towards educating myself. I wasn't a business owner, neither was I an investor. I was an employee, which is also an advantage. That way, you get to keep the security of a job while you learn the language and requirements for wealth. The key is to begin where you are until you're ready to take the fast vehicle, but first you need to educate yourself.

My goal was first to become financially free in ten years or less and with that goal and a plan, a strategy, and timeline, I went to work. The problem is that most people are trying to get rich using their own money, but if you want to get rich you need it learn how to use other people's money – leverage.

To start your wealth journey you need to move from working for ordinary or active income (income from a job) to working for income producing investment assets, because ordinary income is the highest taxable income in most countries and it is also the only income with little or no leverage. You have to exchange your most important asset for it – your time. With active income conditional on you investing your time, you will be limited in how much you can make because someone else gets to decide what they believe your value is. With investment income, the only limit is that placed in your imagination by yourself. Like me, you might have to begin with a job earning an active income, but the important thing is to quickly convert your earnings to savings and invest in assets that create multiple sources of passive income.

There is no get rich quick magic wand. One of the worst mistakes people make is trying to become wealthy quickly. Anything achieved too soon, too freely without the process is often lost. Wealth is anything but quick. It's not a sprint; it's a marathon. And the key to understanding this lies in managing your mind,-focus, thoughts and emotions. Financial intelligence is emotional intelligence. If you can manage and control your mind, then you have one of the qualities for dealing with money and investing. If you can't control your mind, you will be attracted to get rich quick or wrong schemes that will push you further away from achieving freedom.

Property investing

The rich and wealthy will always invest in property, and if you study their lives you'll observe there is one commonality – they make or protect their wealth in property. I discovered this when I began my financial education, and it was this knowledge that further enhanced my desire for property. Those who have something you don't (but wish to), know something you don't, and it's is your responsibility to find out what they know, study them, and replicate their success.

Building wealth is a long term process, and with the leverage options available I chose property and business. I understand paper assets and commodities, but I'm not passionate about either at this stage in my life.

One reason I don't invest much in other vehicles is because one of the first wealth strategies I learned before I began my journey was to never invest in something I don't want to know a lot about – and I pass the same advice to you. Don't invest in a product, service, business, industry, or area that you have no interest in, or in a business where you don't trust the people who are representing you as advisors.

The secret to achievements is focus: *flourish in one commitment until successful*. Focus is one of the strategies for achieving wealth quickly. When you diversify, you distribute your energy. Diversification is a strategy if you don't have high financial intelligence and don't know what to do; true security is found in focus. If you have a high financial IQ, you should focus instead on diversifying. Billionaire investor Warren Buffett said, 'Diversification is protection against ignorance. It makes little sense if you know what you are doing.' I have two views on diversification. If you have good financial intelligence, I would advocate lots of concentration on the investment vehicles you know a lot about and to invest for the long term. For everyone else, diversification could be a safer approach, especially where you have a limited financial IQ and don't intend to expand your wisdom.

The success of property investing is hugely dependent on knowledge of the market (including the trends) in the geographical area and demand-supply economics. It's only financially viable to invest if the property is located in an area with jobs and educational institutions with further long term growth potential. This is why property investing requires constant and never ending continuous improvement in your education – you begin and remain a student with property investing.

Property is technically a slow vehicle to creating wealth, but the leverage options make it attractive. It requires staying power, and you should see it as a long term investment plan. I have a bias towards property, perhaps because of my experience with buildings prior to retiring from engineering. I understand buildings and construction; my passion and interest in property is stronger than any other investment vehicle. Putting my experience aside, I believe that property is a much easier investment to understand (because we live and work in buildings and on land).

I love property for the following reasons:

- I understand buildings because I worked in building design and construction for fifteen years prior to retiring from engineering.

- I live and work in buildings like many so I am familiar with how a building works.

- I can use debt leverage and I can get wealthy using other people money while I retain complete control and the appreciation in value.

- The banks (and other financial institutions) see it as less risky compared to other investment vehicles and they are happy to be my partner.

- The tax advantages are incomparable to any other investment vehicle.

- The income options and appreciation benefits are exclusive to property alone.

- It's safe and stable if you have the right financial intelligence.

- I can get the highest return compared to any other investment. In most cases an infinite return.

- I can delegate the management responsibility to a property management firm and still retain control.

As with all investments, education is key. Anyone who claims that a particular investment vehicle (including property) will make you wealthy is mistaken. Your financial intelligence and experience of a particular vehicle makes the difference. The onus is on you – you are responsible for your success, not the investment vehicle or product. Every investment is a product, and you shouldn't focus on the product but on the plan. Property is about the plan supporting the deal.

Many people talk about property, but the truth is that until you understand the art of looking out for the best properties, paying the least for them, and maximising your return you might not become wealthy through property. The entrepreneurial attitude is essential with property, otherwise the best opportunities could be missed. Vision is really important with property; you have to learn to see not by sight alone but also through your imagination – seeing opportunities, possibilities, and inevitabilities. With imagination and insight, you can see ways in which a property's value can be increased. Property requires solid financial education, good financing and property management.

CHAPTER 17

DOING MORE WITH LESS: USING LEVERAGE TO GET AHEAD

Leverage is the reason some people become rich and others do not.
— *Robert Kiyosaki*

everage is one of the most important words you need to understand if you're going to become wealthy. The definitions in some dictionaries are somewhat misleading and don't provide the right picture, especially in a financial context, so let me provide a definition that will accord with the theme of the book. *Leverage is simply 'advantage'*, anything that gives you additional help over what may have been possible. It's a multiplier and offers you the ability to use your available resources to maximise or increase your potential return on the investment of your time, energy, effort, money or wisdom. It isn't limited to the use of borrowed funds in the purchase of an asset.

When I emigrated to London, I applied the principles of leverage. I knew that my new environment could help me achieve my goals more quickly. The opportunities in London – access to more knowledge, the right people, equal opportunities and a platform to launch my dreams – provided the leverage I needed . We use leverage every day. Paying someone to fly us from one destination to another, eating in a restaurant instead of cooking ourselves, learning from a successful mentor – these are forms of leverage. Leverage isn't limited to money (it is a good form of leverage but not the most important).

Financial freedom is made easier through the use of multiple forms of leverage – relationships, successful people's time, experience, wisdom and other people's money. The more you can apply to help you achieve your dreams, the better. There are two major forms of leverage you must apply in your life to become wealthy – *wisdom and debt*. Wisdom is the most important form of leverage because it helps you see, understand and apply other leverage options.

Wisdom

Your willingness to use the leverage of wisdom is the biggest contributor to making your dreams a reality. Wisdom is a broad topic, but I'm talking about financial wisdom. The ability to solve financial problems through wisdom (whether yours or someone else's) separates those who are financially free from the rest. It's not what you know – *knowledge* – it's what you do with what you know – *wisdom*.

Financial wisdom is the ability to identify and pursue financial opportunities; it's also the ability to solve any financial problem or challenge. With wisdom you can see far beyond what would be ordinarily possible because it lets you see by vision not sight alone. The traditional way to increase your financial wisdom is through your experience, but this is the slowest way to gain wisdom. Leveraging the wisdom and experience of others offers a shortcut, and this is the most important reason for my financial freedom. I chose to study, learn and model myself on other successful people.

One reason I stress the importance of wisdom is because wealth creation and retention is heavily dependent on understanding taxes, law, accounting, debt, markets, trends, cycles, history and the ability to look into the future and make an educated assessment of what might be. Wealth (like engineering, medical sciences, law, and accounting) has a unique language. There is a vocabulary to wealth. If you have

124

ever travelled to a foreign country but couldn't speak the language, you probably found communication challenging. In a similar way, if you don't know the vocabulary of wealth, it will be difficult to understand, communicate or apply the principles of wealth in your life.

Wisdom leverage begins with the study of the vocabulary (words) so you can communicate effectively. Words help you interpret and express, and if you can do neither your interactions will be limited. If you want to be wealthy, discipline yourself to make it a study, because without wisdom, failure looms. The first and best investments are those you make in yourself so one of your goals should be directed towards your personal development. If you want to take charge of your life, my recommendation is to adopt this and make a habit of investing daily in yourself. Increase your wisdom because the size of your future will seldom exceed the level of your investment in your personal development and growth.

Debt

If you want to be wealthy and rich, you have to learn how to use debt – investment debt. You aren't supposed to use your own money to get financially free if you can avoid it. You are supposed to use other people's money (your bank's or investors) in the form of debt. This is how the rich get richer; they use debt leverage. Investment debt is simply debt you get into primarily for the purpose of creating bigger and better opportunities to serve more people by solving more problems and creating more value for others. In return, using such debt helps you increase your wealth, but more importantly the debt is paid for by others. Investment debt should only be considered for the primary purpose of multiplying capital and creating more wealth. Debt financing is not available to all investment vehicles but it's required in property investing. Financially intelligent investors only take on the necessary level of debt required to secure a viable investment if they're certain of a profit. The quantity of debt secured by the investor should be in relation to the investor's level of financial intelligence because debt is like a loaded gun – it can protect or take life.

I only take on debt for a property investment if my due diligence appraisal confirms I can successfully generate a profit and passive income from the investment. If the calculated return on the investment only meets the minimum value required to compensate for the risk, I don't take on debt. Also, the level of debt I take on is proportional to my financial experience with debt. I'm cautious about taking on debt because debt only respects wisdom.

For my first investment, I had £30,000 but by using debt leverage, I was able to purchase a property of £215,000. The two forms of leverage discussed in this chapter were applied – wisdom and debt. Through financial wisdom I knew that no financial institution would give me a loan to invest in paper assets (stocks or bonds), commodities or a business, but I knew banks love property and would easily loan the amount because they perceive it to be tangible, less risky, and also because it is really their asset and they make a lot of money from it. It took the investment of time in study for me to understand the various investment options and their advantages.

Secondly, I knew that no other investment vehicle offered the same tax advantages, leverage options, asset protection, return on investment or opportunity to become wealthy. With property investing I could invest £30,000, get it back tax free after two years, maintain my income flow and increase my net worth by over a quarter of a million pounds during that period. All created from nothing. This is the power of leverage (debt leverage) – the ability to use other people's resources to achieve your desired outcomes.

At this point you might be thinking debt leverage is risky, and you might not be wrong (depending on your financial IQ). It is if you have little or no wisdom. We tend to see things as impossible, difficult or complicated, but if you have wisdom, it isn't. Ignorance makes leverage risky, but if you have good wisdom, you have control, which reduces uncertainty. The key is to not to invest in anything you don't want to know a lot about or have a passion for. Without passion, wisdom is limited, and without wisdom, failure is inevitable.

Leverage isn't risky if you invest in assets you have control over. With my property investments, I have control over the operations and management, and because of this I control the income created, not the market conditions. If you want more control, increase your financial intelligence. The key is to start small and stay small until your wisdom increases.

The rich way

If you want to be wealthy, you must follow the rich way. First invest in your financial education to gain wisdom so you can take advantage of all available wealth strategies, next adopt all leverage options (specially debt via other people's money) to acquire passive income generating assets (preferably assets that appreciate consistently with time) to generate income and then reinvest the returns (income) from each investment to create multiple sources of income.

One reason many are still financially dependent is because they are trying to do it on their own without leverage. Most people try to use the longer route to financial freedom. We have been conditioned to work for money until we retire and can enjoy what we have spent a lifetime saving, but this is a slow vehicle and also an unsustainable approach to wealth.

With financial leverage, you can become wealthy more quickly if you understand how to use it. Leverage finds its integrity when used with good financial intelligence. If you don't have integrity, debt leverage should be avoided at all cost.

People who suffer losses in property don't lose money because property investing entails risk, they lose money because they fail to learn and apply the principles of property analysis, investment and financial management. Secondly many lose because they buy to make an immediate profit; you need to buy and hold property that will provide positive cash flow (income) each month. Never invest in a property simply because of its potential future appreciation.

Part 6

PLAYING THE GAME TO WIN

CHAPTER 18

MONEY: MASTER IT

Money is a terrible master but an excellent servant.
— *Phineas Taylor Barnum*

Money, like time, is an emotional subject for many. When we talk about money people either have a positive or negative feeling towards it. But money is simply a means for measuring the level of value you create for others using your knowledge, skills, talent, gifts and wisdom.

It's a reward you receive for solving problems and creating value for others. What you do with it, how you use it, and how you think towards it decides the experience you have with it. Shakespeare once said, *Nothing is either good or bad but thinking makes it so.* Money is neither good nor bad, it's just money, and it becomes what your think it is. If you believe it's a tool for creating great experiences for people you care about, you will be drawn to ideas on how you can attract it and things you could do with it to make a difference to others. On the other hand, if you believe it's evil, you will associate little or no value to it and therefore won't actively seek to be wealthy. Almost everything we do is connected to money in some way, and if you wish to become wealthy you must have an understanding of it. Our behaviour towards money is evident in how we use it, and it is this attitude that has kept people in lack. To break this downward cycle, you have to begin with an understanding of money.

The average adult spends seventy per cent of their waking day (ten to twelve hours, including travel) working for money, and from the age of eighteen would work for fifty years for money. You'd think that if we will spend more than fifty years of our lives doing something, we'd spend some time learning something about it, but few people have been educated on the use of money. Most people spend all the money their hands touch because they haven't been taught the purpose of money. And most people spend everything they earn because they don't understand the value, brevity and purpose of time.

Money is more important than most people want to acknowledge. If you make a list of all your dreams and goals, you may be surprised to realise that seventy per cent of the items on your list will require money or will be related to money in some way or another. With money, your dreams can become reality, you can meet your financial commitments to your family, you can complete your purpose on the earth, and you can help others create and experience a more fulfilled life. You can take care of those who can't take care of themselves and you can contribute to change the world in a positive way.

Where does it all go?

If you study money and understand it and are willing to apply wisdom, good judgement and calculated risk in using it, this will help you achieve your financial dream. Start by accepting that money is simply an idea, and develop a positive mental attitude, philosophy and belief towards it. As an idea, it can be developed into a thought, a feeling and a result. The way you use the idea will determine how well you create, protect and multiply wealth.

The value of money is based on what the world believes it's worth. Most of the world's money is invested in assets other than cash, and in many cases the transactions are based on credit and debt – neither of which are tangible or concrete – they're simply ideas. For example, say I deposit £10,000 in my bank as savings. The bank then lends ten times the amount (£100,000) to a borrower. The borrower purchases an investment that produces a cash flow of £25 each week, and from the £100 received each month they pay for a number of business expenses. The total transactions represent £110,100 originating from my original £10,000 investment. This demonstrates that what we think of as money is simply an idea.

The value of money varies in proportion to where and how it is to be used. Ten thousand pounds in the hands of someone who places little value on money will be spent quickly, most probably on liabilities that meet their instant gratification needs but add nothing of substance to their lives. The same quantity of money in the hands of someone who is financially intelligent will be invested wisely and could potentially create an infinite return on the initial investment, demonstrating that money is as valuable as the choices and decisions we make with it.

Your income source

Money is obtained predominantly through an income, a salary or wages earned from a job. All incomes are not equal. Some make you wealthy and free while others make you secure and dependent. You must understand the various income sources, but more importantly you must know the income source that will guide you towards financial freedom, because this is where you want to focus most of your energy, time and effort. Most people work hard, and some earn high incomes, but they are still financially dependent because they're working for the wrong income.

There are two main income sources – ordinary or earned income (active income) and investment (passive and portfolio) income.

Earned or active income is the income you have to work for. You exchange your time, energy, effort, wisdom and presence for it. If you don't work, you don't earn. It's unleveraged income and has a single point of failure. With earned income, you are a servant to money because you must perform specific services though labour to have it. Active income includes business income and personal income through wages, salaries, tips, and commission. If you want to accumulate wealth, let it be known that you rarely get rich by working for money. I know there is a handful of company executives who have high incomes, but they are exceptions, not the rule. You must put it into context by taking into account the number of people in the work force – this is probably two or three billion people compared to the few thousands that are paid an executive's salary. Working for money doesn't make you wealthy. You might have a high salary or wage but I am unconcerned with how much you earn today. Show me how much of it you'll have ten years from today and I'll tell you how much you earned today. Earning is only the first step in maximising money as a resource.

Investment income is the income created by an investment or asset. The investment works for you and provides an income. You can get your investment income by saving part of your earned income and using the saved amount to acquire an asset that will work by generating income. The two types of investment income are portfolio and passive income. Portfolio income is the income you make from your investments, dividends, interest, capital gains and royalties. In some cases, it's income from the appreciation in the value of your assets. Passive income is income earned on a regularly basis (daily, monthly or annually) with little or no investment of your time, energy or effort. For example, the royalties I get from each purchase of this book is an example of a portfolio income while the income I receive from my rental properties is passive income. Both come from my investments assets but they provide two types of income. In other words, my investment income is one I create without being materially involved and without having to continuously exchange my time, energy, focus or wisdom. The income is created whether I work or not – this is money working for me.

Income from investment assets is better than income from a job because:

- You don't have to exchange your most important asset for it – time.
- You also don't have to exchange your energy, effort, wisdom or presence continuously.

- Your money is working for you instead of you working for money. Money becomes your servant not your master.

- It offers better tax advantages and it provides better opportunities for using debt leverage.

- It provides a quicker path to wealth.

Playing defence

Wealth is created not only by playing offence but also by playing defence. Both active and investment income sources are derived from playing offence, but there are a few defence income sources worth learning. Income is not only generated when you earn; income is also generated when you defer or reduce consumption. Here are two options for your consideration:

Negotiation: Study the life of the rich and you'll realise they are masters of negotiation. They know how to get what they want at a price they want. Negotiation is crucial if you want to be wealthy. It should be a part of your everyday life and is critical for business success. When I was a young boy, we did most of our shopping in the market. I spent some time around traders and I love the art of negotiation. I like to negotiate when I can and if the circumstances are right. Think that's cheap? Well, I'm not alone – the likes of Donald J Trump, Warren Buffet, Denise Coates, Mark Zukerberg, Chan Laiwa and many of the other billionaire investors and business people in the same group are rich because of their ability to identify great deals and buy them for much less than their true worth. If you feel ashamed when negotiating, you are not a good steward of money. It's not the money you make, it is the money you keep that makes you wealthy, and negotiation is one way to keep what you have. It is the money you have now that you use to create your future, not the money yet to come.

Delayed purchase: The ability to wait forty-eight to seventy-two hours before any major purchase (especially any wants and liabilities that aren't necessities) has the potential to create more financially free people than any other wealth plan. Instant gratification has robbed more people of their financial destiny than any known element. We generally spend more on our wants than we do on our needs, and in many cases most of our purchases are made emotionally rather than rationally. By increasing the time before any purchase, you allow yourself the time to test the emotions associated with the desire. You significantly increase your odds of becoming wealthy by diverting money into your investment fund instead of spending it. The delayed purchase strategy should generally be used for all purchases, but especially when buying your wants and luxury items.

Money – what to do with it?

You can invest it, save it or spend it. Financial intelligence is evident by the approach you adopt. The first rule in the wealth creation journey is the principle pay yourself first. Before you pay for any of the expenses on your financial statement, set aside a designated percentage of what your earn for yourself – to save and invest.

If you're an employee, your options are limited because your taxes are paid first. The first line of expense for most people is normally taxes, but you can still pay yourself first by making contributions to a pension scheme. This is especially recommended when there's a matched contribution from your employer. Doing this will mean you pay yourself first using your pre-tax income. However, a pension scheme isn't an investment plan, it's a tax deferred saving plan.

Your first line of expense after tax should be to yourself based on the allocations in the 65-35 plan discussed earlier. This habit (if adhered to consistently) will not only make you a millionaire, it will also help you build good wealth. Doing this helps you with the discipline required to live within your means. We all want to save and invest but our monthly expenses and responsibilities often get first pass on our pay and we're left with no option but to save what's left over – which is usually not much.

When you pay yourself first, you're mentally establishing investing and saving as a priority. You're telling yourself *you have first priority in your life*. Paying yourself first encourages sound financial habits. Most people spend their money in the following order: bills – fun – saving.

Unsurprisingly, there's usually little left over for investing. But the wealth strategy is to reverse the order by investing first and dealing with other necessities next.

The best way to develop the pay-yourself first habit and lifestyle is to make the process as painless as possible by automation. Make arrangements for the money to be taken from your pay cheque before you receive it so you'll never know it's missing.

Invest or save

Saving is a slow means to the end, while investing is a fast means to the end, but if you grew up like me you were probably taught and encouraged to save money. It was probably sound wealth creation advice prior to my birth, but with all the changes that have taken place globally (especially over the past forty years), it's no longer sound advice. You can't save your way to wealth; you need a better plan.

Saving money to get wealthy is like going into a battlefield with an obsolete fighting strategy (and with no leverage) like Goliath did in his battle against David. Goliath went into battle with a sword, spear and shield, but David chose a sling and four stones, a powerful choice of weaponry that he could use with accuracy from a distance without getting close to his opponent. With a different choice of weaponry David would have been the underdog, but with a sling in his hand he now had the advantage- he had leverage. In ancient warfare, the armies consisted of cavalry (chariots and horse riders), heavy infantry (armed foot soldiers) and artillery (archers and slingers). Goliath came to battle on the assumption that he would be fighting according to terms of short range combat – foot soldier against foot soldier but David had other ideas. The famous battle was a fight between a foot soldier and an artillery fighter which in today's times would have been similar to a knife and gun fight. David's choice of weaponry rendered Goliath's weapon obsolete and this cost Goliath his life.

In a similar way, many are trying to achieve their financial dreams using outdated, unleveraged and obsolete approaches to wealth. Saving is not investing. When you save, the value and purchasing power of your saved money (in currency form) declines in value because of inflation and other factors, but if you invest, your money compounds.

Once you have your emergency fund secure as discussed in earlier chapters, you should try as much as possible not to actively save. By actively I mean saving for the long term. It's OK to save passively (for the short term) with a purpose and a goal in mind. Each time you save you should have a timeline, a strategy and a plan for investing the saved funds. It's my opinion that anyone saving for more than a year is missing out on a lot of great opportunities for wealth creation. Remember that capital isn't a prerequisite for wealth creation. Most people blame a lack of resources (money) for their financial position, but it isn't the lack of resources that is the problem, it's their lack of resourcefulness. If you have passion, focus, enthusiasm, drive and persistence, you can start to build your financial future – you simply need to be creative and resourceful.

The millionaire code

You know you're poor if you think a million is a lot. The word 'millionaire' rings a tone, a nice one I have to admit, but perhaps not as nice as 'billionaire'. Millionaire has been used a benchmark for describing wealth or prosperity, and so much has been written about becoming a millionaire that it has done two things: it has confined many to a new middle class way of thought – seeking security. It has also discouraged a lot of people from the true message, which is freedom. There are usually two distinct groups of emotions expressed by people. One is the emotions of scarcity, fear, lack, security and comfort while other is abundance, freedom, prosperity and benevolence. The millionaire mindset is one of security and comfort rather than freedom.

To be free, you have to think abundance rather than scarcity, but you mustn't use the million benchmark to limit your ability to create and dream. Nor should you let it distract you from beginning your journey. Many people fail to get off ground zero simply because they look at where they find themselves and contrast it against the millionaire yardline and they're discouraged. The millionaire's club is only a stopping point on your wealth journey. Make it a goal and a stopping point on your journey and not the launch pad.

You don't need to be a millionaire or have a lot of money to be financially free – I have demonstrated this isn't true. I didn't become financially free as a millionaire; I was financially free when I had sufficient passive income created by my investments capable of meeting my monthly expenses without me having to work. I was free not because I had a million pounds or a million pound net worth, but because I never had to work again (except by choice) as my income-expense ratio (wealth ratio) was greater than one. This was the starting point, and my focus since achieving my freedom has been on increasing my wealth ratio whilst increasing my net worth through multiple sources of income. You don't need to be wealthy to get started, but you need to start if you wish to be wealthy. Begin your journey first and start working on a strategy for multiplication. Don't let the millionaire myth or other false ideas stop you from building your wealth.

CHAPTER 19

THE GOOD PLAN:
LIVE A DEBT FREE LIFE

The greatest enemy of financial well-being is not poverty but debt.
— *Kent Nerburn*

To be financially free you have to adopt a policy called the GOOD policy: Get Out Of Debt. I am referring to personal debt or any other kind of bad debt (debts taken out for liabilities). Debt can be your friend or your enemy. If secured against assets that decline in value such as personal possessions, personal items or accessories or luxury items (planes, boats, cars, clothing), it's risky and is bad debt. But if the debt is secured against assets that increase in value while generating an income, it's good debt (investment debt) and can help you become wealthy.

Being in personal debt (bad debt) is not the problem. It is a symptom of a problem, and in many case most people are trying to fix the symptom but they don't understand the problem. Without fixing the problem, it remains and continues to cause havoc. Being in bad debt is not due to a lack of money or not earning enough. It's a failure of understanding of the purpose of money and its appropriate

141

management(Lack of wisdom), a result of poor money paradigms and habits but more importantly, it is a self-image problem. Reccurring or long term debt issues must be dealt with within first, not without. Most people try to deal with their debt issue by focusing on external activities (effect) rather than dealing with internal or subconscious issue (causes). Debt can only be permanently resolved by changing your self-image, the way you think and increasing your wisdom. This will lead to a change in feelings and actions followed by a change of habits and paradigms, behaviour and, finally, lifestyle.

Because of the limited amount of financial education provided in schools, many people aren't fully aware of the pitfalls associated with debt and fall far into debt before realising that it's too late. If you're willing to accept complete responsibility for your personal predicaments and follow the guidelines that follow, you will be out of debt in a short time.

The plan

To get out of debt you need you need a vision. The vision must be converted into a goal and the goal converted into a plan. Depending on your specific personal circumstances, the timeframe will vary, but any goal can be achieved with discipline, consistency, patience, sacrifice, focus and effort. There are four essential stages to go through if you wish to completely eliminate all personal debt from your life. First you must quantify it, then control it. Next you must reduce it, and finally eliminate it. But before you begin you have to accept complete responsibility for the position in which you find yourself. One of the reasons we often get into and remain in debt is because we are not accountable, and this is a necessary pre-requisite to getting out of debt.

Quantify it: The first thing you must do is to quantify how much you owe. This is usually what most people shy away from, and where we lie to ourselves and our loved ones. You must start with the truth if you ever want to get out of debt. Winston Churchill, the former British Prime Minster, once said, 'The truth is incontrovertible, malice may attack it, ignorance may deride it, but in the end; there it is'. You can lie to yourself and others; you can pretend you have no debt but eventually it rises to the top, like cream. You can't keep your debt secrets buried for ever. You have to set them free and it starts with documentation – capture your debts in writing. You can only manage what you can measure. Prepare a detailed statement of all the debt owed (including interests) and with this you can start the journey to get you out. Start with an inventory of debts – the names of each creditor, the total amount owed, the total payoff balance (including any interest) and the monthly repayment amount.

When you've finished, add up all the amounts from each debtor to get the *total debt amount*. This will be used for setting your debt elimination goal. At this point I should point out that you should separate your mortgage from the other debts you owe. It's still bad debt because you have to pay for it to live in it, but your home mortgage debt will be eliminated differently.

For all other debts, lets capture some essential information in writing. On a new page in your journal write down 'debt elimination strategy'.

Then write out the first creditor owed, the total amount owed and the minimum amount due each month. Next, work out the total time it will take to repay all the debt. You calculate this by dividing the total amount owed by the minimum payment. For example if you owed £12,000 for a home improvement loan and the minimum payment each month was £400, it would take you 30 months to pay it off (£12,000/£400), if you maintained the same repayment amount.

Now with the timeline for the first debt account established, repeat the same process for all your other debts. This will give you a timeline for eliminating all of your debt which is important because your goal of becoming debt free is only complete when you set a deadline. You will understand the importance of this exercise when you get to the fourth and final stage of the debt elimination state.

Control it: The next thing you have to do is stop any further debt increase. Just like you would stop digging if you found yourself in a deep hole, you have to stop digging yourself into a deeper financial pit; you must stop accruing more debt. This might be difficult in your present circumstances but until you stop, you can't get out. This starts by changing your thinking and habits. If you are in debt (perhaps with the exception of a mortgage or school loan), you certainly have poor money habits and it has to stop. I know that there are exceptions (for emergencies or other unforeseen circumstances) to this but I am not dealing with those here, I am focused on debts that have accrued due to lack of accountability and sound financial planning.

Getting rid of your credit cards is recommended to avoid the temptation in using it to get further into debt. With your cards gone, the temptation to use your credit card to fund a lifestyle you haven't earned and don't deserve will be reduced. If you have a lot of debt but are unwilling to eliminate all your cards, you are like a boat that is fifty feet from Niagara Falls with no motor – your downfall is inevitable. Choose the new life; choose freedom by getting rid of their shackles that have held you down too long. If you're unable to do this, you should consider professional help – contact one of your local debt services or a reputable local non-profit organisation. The temptation we have is to save one card for emergencies, but in many cases what we call an emergency is really a failure on our part to be creative when we find ourselves in an unwanted position. Emergencies (excluding medical injuries and emergencies) rarely occur frequently, and if they are in your life often, it's a sign of poor planning. Until you're willing to burn your boats and decide you will stop retreating back into your comfort zone, it might be difficult to get out of debt.

Reduce it: Next you have to reduce the debt you owe, and this begins by separating your needs from your wants. In the majority of cases, people get into debt for their wants rather than their needs. There are fewer cases of people in debt because they had to buy their groceries on credit cards than there are people who paid for luxury accessories and items they knew they couldn't afford. To successfully reduce your debt, it is best to start paying for everything in cash so you are fully aware of how much you are spending every time, but also so you don't overspend. Credit cards should only be used if you intend to pay the full balance completely upon receipt of the bill; otherwise credit cards, and store cards are invitations to trouble. By paying with cash you will be more accountable and aware of your actions and will start asking yourself tough questions like 'Is this need or a want?' or 'Is this really important right now'?

Approximately eighty per cent of the money (after your basic needs such as shelter, food and clothing) you spend is usually for your wants not your needs. When you find you are trying to purchase a want, simply increase the time between purchases. Desire always follows focus. If you shift your focus and attention away from the item, your desire will reduce and this will help in diverting any impulse purchases. If you are in debt, you should be spending little or nothing on your wants (non-essentials) or luxury items until you are completely out of debt.

There are a few other methods for reducing your debt such as renegotiating your interest rates or shopping around to find a better deal with another provider.

Eliminate it: There are two primary ways to eliminate your debts. Earn more so you can pay more towards your debt or spend less so you can also allocate more towards your debt. My recommendation is to do both. If you are in bad debt you have no justification to live beyond your means, especially if you also spend money on non-essential items such as your wants. This is simply a point of integrity and responsibility; the keeping up with the Joneses attitude does you no favours.

The elimination stage is where you get to use the passive income fund identified in the 65-35 plan. The ten per cent assigned to your passive fund will need to be assigned to your debts. Earlier you documented your debts together with the minimum payment required each month. The minimum payment has to be paid each month and should be funded from your expenses budget allowance (65% of your net income). Next, your passive income allowance (10% of your net income) should be assigned to your debt account. The plan is to direct all your passive income allowance to one creditor account until it is fully paid off and then you move to the next credit account. You repeat this process until all your debts are paid off in full.

Let's look at an example:

We'll assume that your monthly net income is £2,000 and you're £93,000 in debt (£12,000, £13,000, £28,000 and £40,000 on four creditor accounts) and the minimum monthly payments on all four creditor accounts (your debts) are £700 (£400, £80, £120, £100 respectively). Your new debt elimination plan will be to allocate

£900 (10% of your net income + the minimum monthly payment) towards your debt accounts. The 10% (£200) part of the monthly debt reduction amount should be allocated to one debt account while the minimum monthly payment is paid to all debt accounts according to the minimum amounts required for each account. The key is to start with one account until it is fully paid off, then once the first debt is eliminated, redirect the 10% passive income allowance and the minimum payment you were making to the eliminated account to the next debt account. Continue in this fashion until all your debts are eliminated.

For this elimination process to work there are two things you must do – ensure you continue to make the minimum monthly payments on all the accounts, and secondly (but more importantly) don't create any more debt.

There are various ways to choose the first account to pay off. I suggest that you start with the one with the smallest debt so you can taste progress and victory quickly. You will see from the GOOD plan that all your debts are eliminated quickly, so I am not too concerned about the debts with high interest rates but, you can choose your debt elimination priority to suit you . Earlier in the chapter you quantified the timeline for paying off each of your debts by dividing the total debt owed on a single account by the minimum payment. In the example used earlier, one of the debt accounts was £12,000 and the monthly minimum payment was £400, which meant that it would take thirty months to eliminate the debt completely. Let's compare the normal repayment method with the alternative (passive income allocation) elimination method to see the difference.

In the alternative method, you would assign £200 (10% of your net income) and the minimum payment (400) to one account which would be £600 for this account. Therefore, it would take you one year and seven months instead of two and a half years to eliminate this debt (Account 1).

Applying the same comparison to the remaining debt accounts:

- Account 2: The debt will be paid off in 1 years and 8 months instead of 13.5 years

- Account 3: The debt will be paid off in 2 years and 7 months instead of 19.5 years.
- Account 4: The debt will be paid off in 3 years and 8 months instead of 33 years and 4 months.

Can you now see the importance and advantage of focusing your passive income towards one account rather than diversifying it across all accounts? With the suggested debt elimination method it would take you half (or less) the time to get completely out of debt. The key is consistency. Once the first debts is cleared, you redirect the money paid (the minimum payment on the cleared accounts and the 10% passive investment portion) to the next creditor account and you keep compounding this until the final creditor account is paid off completely.

Focus is very important for success and wealth but also for eliminating debt. For those who are unable to apply the 65-35 plan (wealth budget plan) and are using the secure budget plan, it is still important that you follow this process. Although you can't assign 10% of your net income, you should calculate what the amount would be and then apply the offence income creation strategy (increase your means by increasing your disposable income) since the defence approach (living below your means) could be difficult at this point for you. You do this by increasing your income through a different source from your main job (perhaps through a part time job) but the net income earned from the second source should be at least 10% of your regular income because you'll be allocating this to your debt plan. You must endeavour to do the best you can to follow this recommendation irrespective of your financial condition, otherwise you won't be able to eliminate your debts.

With your general debts eliminated, let's move to your mortgage debt.

Mortgage debt

A lot of people make the all too common mistake, popularised in recent years, of thinking that their home is their best asset and will become their retirement security. Although your home could be your biggest investment, and the value of your house could increase over time, that doesn't make it an asset. For a start, the value of something is not based on opinion but on what someone is willing to pay for it in the present – not the future. To ascertain if your home is an asset, you have to ask yourself how much equity you have in it today – not tomorrow – and also what it's costing you each month to own it. In truth, it costs much more than the purchase price to buy, maintain and operate a home each year, but the ongoing operational and maintenance costs are rarely taken into account by many when evaluating the investment overall. You are left with mortgage interests, taxes, insurance, repairs, renovations, improvements, all of which over time add up to a significant amount. Your home is only an asset when it costs you nothing and if it provides you with an income (profit) each month/year. If it doesn't, your home is a liability and therefore you must also eliminate your mortgage debt.

Once you have successfully paid off all other debts, you will be accustomed to the new lifestyle of the 65-35 plan and will have formed the habits of making the monthly minimum payments and assigning ten per cent of your net income towards your debt account. You must maintain this lifestyle and habit because you will need to allocate the total amount paid each month towards your mortgage.

In the earlier example, your monthly debt elimination amount was £900 (10% of your net income + the minimum monthly payments). Therefore, this £900 will be allocated towards your mortgage. This is essential, but before going further, you need to understand the thirty year mortgage cycle. Most mortgages are taken out for thirty to thirty-five years which is one of the biggest rip offs in the housing industry. Very few mortgage institution explain the long term financial benefits of a shorter loan repayment period because doing so will reduce the profits they make from interest payments. This is a financial chain people freely (by choice) allow institutions to place around their lives due to their lack of financial intelligence. A thirty to thirty-five years year loan is OK for investment loans and mortgages because you are using debt leverage (other people's money) to get rich and you want to maximize your cash flow income each month, but you should never sign up for a thirty to thirty-five year home mortgage if you can afford to make higher monthly repayments.

On average homeowners move or re-mortgage every seven to ten years, and the banks and the government have capitalised on this to their benefit. Mortgage loans are calculated in such a way that the institution gets as much as they can in interest before the seven to ten year period. In most cases when people sign up for a thirty year mortgage they barely pay off the principal amount during the first ten years before they decide to re-finance to buy a bigger house, and then the whole process starts all over again and so the principal amount owed is fractionally paid off. There is a way around this, and this is where your debt elimination plan will come in handy. The quicker you pay off your home loan, the more you increase the equity you have in your home and your net worth.

To eliminate your home mortgage debt, the first thing you should do is go back to the lending institution and ask for your mortgage terms to be changed to a ten to fifteen year loan. Once this is changed your monthly payment will increase. Let assume that your monthly mortgage repayment was previously £800 and with the change you are now required to pay £1,200. You already have £900 each month from your elimination account (from the earlier example) so you can allocate £400 to cover your new mortgage amount which will leave you with a £500 balance in your debt elimination fund.

Next you should make an extra 10% payment on your new monthly mortgage; most institutions accept this additional payment of 10% each month, or a single annual payment – but check with your lender first. The extra 10% monthly payment (or one single annual payment) will mean you make one extra monthly payment each year. This could save you between five to seven years on your mortgage term and as much as 20-30% on the total money paid on interest on your mortgage loan. But make sure it goes towards your principal, not the total loan amount. One way to check this is by looking at your mortgage statement to make sure that they are deducting the extra payments from the principal. Some banks don't automatically allocate the extra payments made to your principal debt. By making an extra payment, you reduce your loan term and you can completely eliminate your mortgage debt within eight years instead of fifteen – can you believe it?

Guess what? It's not over yet. You allocated £120 (10% of your new mortgage monthly payment) from your debt fund, leaving you with a balance of £380. Some banks and mortgage institutions won't allow you to pay more than 10% of your monthly mortgage payment as additional payments so you will have to divert this £380 into a separate account. I recommend you use an instant access an individual saving account with the best terms. Assuming you save £380 each month, after four years you would have £16,720 (without any interest). With this you can make a one off lump sum payment on your mortgage which could clear your mortgage debt completely.

With this extra discipline and work on your part you could be debt free within four years instead of thirty by following the debt elimination strategy. I know what you want to say – *impossible*. The proof of the pudding is in the eating, so why not try it? The numbers don't lie.

Follow the steps above and you will be debt free in a short time. Many people fall back into their old habit of spending once they've successfully paid off all their debts, and this must be avoided at all costs. Once your debts are cleared, you should redirect the money (the minimum payment on all accounts, the 10% passive investment portion and your mortgage monthly payment) towards your active investment fund account immediately.

Using the same example, this would mean that you have £1,700 (£700 from the initial minimum payments + £200 from your 10% passive fund + £800 from your initial mortgage repayment) which can be redirected towards investing. If you do, then you will be investing over 85% of your net income towards your future, and this habit alone will make you wealthy beyond your wildest dreams.

CHAPTER 20

GIVE IT ALL:
THE ULTIMATE KEY

Don't wait. The time will never be just right.

— *Napoleon Hill*

Very few associate giving with wealth and sadly few see it as a condition for prosperity or necessity for living abundantly. Some think that giving is a luxury they can't afford or a burden they don't need. It is often seen as a loss, and many only give when they have enough left. My thoughts on the subject of giving is deeply rooted in my Christian beliefs and it is nicely captured in the invitation *Give and it will be given to you* (Luke 6:38). Just like I know the law of gravity is infallible with the earth's gravitational field, so is the law of giving.

It is my deep conviction that wealth and giving are interwoven and inseparable. True wealth is incomplete without the art and lifestyle of giving – tithes, gifts and gratitude. The ability and willingness to give personally and financially through philanthropy is a fundamental part of prosperity.

If you study the lives of some of the wealthiest people who have ever lived, including those living today, you would observe a common denominator – they gave or have committed to give away a vast amount of the wealth they created, for example, Andrew Carnegie, John Templeton, R G LeTourneau, Bill Gates and Warren Buffet. Why did they do this? Well, if you don't share it, the same wealth that brings you joy could also bring you sorrow in your business, personal and family life.

Your desire to become financially free should be connected to a greater purpose or life contribution such as improving the lives of others. For example, it could be so you can help your favourite charity or support your local church or community. Giving is the greatest reason to be wealthy and rich, and one of the major reasons I wanted to become financially free was so I could see how much I could give away in my lifetime. I have been inspired by the lives of some of the greatest givers who lived, many of whom are unknown to the world but who have changed lives through their commitment to giving.

There should be a commitment on your part to give daily, monthly or yearly, and it should be set as a goal to which you apply as much focus and effort to accomplish as becoming wealthy. As we discussed in the earlier chapters, ten per cent of your net income should be set aside towards tithing or charitable giving. Giving has to go beyond an act; it should become a habit and a lifestyle where you don't think about it, you simply do it. To make sure it's done properly, it must start as a goal and it should be supported by a plan and a continuously improved strategy. Start small and the more you practice, the better you become.

Giving is investing and should be approached with the same intelligent standards as you would apply to any entrepreneurial or business activity. It's important to give, but if all you did was give without thinking beyond the present, you may be creating a greater dependency than helping in the long run. Give money, but also give time, energy, wisdom and opportunities.

You should never give:

- To be paid back
- Out of obligation
- For the selfish pleasure of spending it

- To boost your ego
- For tax advantages

Give because you have a need to give. Deriving personal benefits from giving isn't wrong. In fact, you should find joy, happiness and pleasure from each experience because the experience from the act cannot be compared to any other thing in the world. A gift is not invalidated by selfish desires such as vanity, guilt or fame, so learn to give whatever your motives might be. If you take your focus occasionally away from getting and instead give, you will find peace and joy flows into your life.

Most people say, 'If I had millions, I would give more' but the truth is if you can't give away £1 when you have £10, you certainly won't give out £100,000 when you have a million. Start with where you are and what you have. Maybe you are already in a deficit financial situation and your reason for not being able to give is based on not having enough. Whilst this might be true, you can still give because no one is too poor to give a little. Give whatever you can. It isn't the amount that counts, it's the heart and discipline. Giving isn't expenditure. It's an investment and has little or nothing to do with your income level – it has more to do with your heart. By applying the 65-35 principle discussed earlier, you make giving a priority before spending.

If you can give it away, you're a master over your money. If you can't, your money is a master over you. The question isn't whether you can afford to give. It's whether you can afford not to.

Say the blessing

History is made every day and it's also being written, and if you have diligently read all of this book and are prepared to put into action what you have learned, you are about to rewrite the remaining chapters of your life, and that thought should get you excited. I know for a fact that today is the poorest you will ever be the rest of your life, but as you get ready for your best life ever, it's also important to remember the source of all good things in your life.

The second part of the giving process, is giving thanks through gratitude. Gratitude is the expression from you that you value the kindness received and the act is the key to increase in any area of life.

The more grateful you are, the more good things you will receive. The mental attitude of gratitude draws you closer to the source through which wealth and good things in life come. Gratitude brings your mind closer to the creative mind of the universe.

Money (and all other material things) alone will not bring you joy unless it's combined with gratitude from a sincere thankful heart. If you can't turn your journey and experience into words of thanksgiving and gratitude, you will develop an aura of pride, and as you know your fall is inevitable with pride. Growing in gifts but not in gratitude is the ultimate failure.

Gratitude is a practice. It's not instinctive. Speak to any teacher, parent or guardian responsible for any child in adolescence, or better still observe a group of teenagers, and you will quickly discover the act of gratitude isn't inborn or natural. Gratitude has to be learned, then you have to make it a practice. Through practice you develop it into a habit, and through repetition it becomes a lifestyle. Gratitude must transcend being an attitude. It has to become an act – a daily experience – because without action it is incomplete. Just like faith is incomplete without works.

- Are you a grateful person? If I interviewed five of the closest people you have in your life, would they described you as a grateful person?

- How often do you express your gratitude? Daily, monthly or yearly?

Do you have grateful habits? If you don't, why not develop a daily gratitude habit and make it part of your daily routine? Start day and end your day in gratitude. Why? – because you can. Life is a fascinating mystery, and each morning you get to see a new day, not because you're brilliant and have earned it, you receive it by grace – we all do. By starting your day with and in gratitude, you acknowledge this grace which helps you set the theme of your day – that of thankfulness.

If you don't consider gratitude to important, imagine waking up tomorrow and the only things you had in your life were the things you were grateful for today. Think about this for a few minutes. Look back at yesterday and consider what you would have been entitled to today based on your level of gratitude. You probably have a busy

154

life, but don't let it be the reason for ingratitude. Make a decision to start anew from today and start by making gratitude a daily experience in your life. Learn to give thanks in all things – good or bad. If you show gratitude for what you already have, you attitude of gratitude will attract into your life what you truly want.

Wealth without gratitude and giving is poverty in the spirit. What will it profit you to gain all the wealth in the world and be unfulfilled? Wealth is not only about anticipation, accumulation and expectation, it's also about appreciation, giving and gratitude.

Habitualise it

Work hard as you want, apply the principles in this book, but without gratitude in the equation, your experience of wealth will be incomplete. Gratitude is the only thing that protects and multiplies wealth. Appreciation and gratitude show your true wealth emotionally, mentally, spiritually and psychologically, and every day you should try to capture at least three gratitude moments from your day. They can and should be little things and needn't be grand events or experiences. They enable you to see how much love and grace you have in your life.

Life is beautiful, and you should treat it like the beautiful gift it is. Every day is worthy of celebration because every day is a present you receive by grace. Decide you will be grateful every day. Don't express gratitude because you get everything you want, rather be grateful because you love and appreciate what you already have – the little things, the big things, the things that have come and gone, but most importantly the things yet to come. Learn to give thanks and celebrate in all things. Don't let your circumstances and events in your life rob you of the joy of gratitude.

If you believe the source of all good things in your life is a product of your effort, you might find it difficult to be grateful at all times. I believe everything is God's by his right of creation. I come into and I will live this world with nothing, so nothing I have is mine by right. I see myself as a steward of God and I know that everything I have was made possible not only through his grace but also through the collaboration and support of others. And for that and many more reasons, I am forever grateful.

Don't live and act like you earned it all yourself. Learn to be grateful for whatever you have. Gratitude is made complete when you see, say, show, and share the blessing. Don't worship the gift and ignore the giver.

Gratitude is the key to true wealth. If you are a grateful person, you will lack nothing in life.

CHAPTER 21

DRAW THE CURTAINS: FINAL THOUGHTS

Freedom is the right to question and change the established way of doing things.
— *Ronald Reagan*

My experience has shown me that while it might be easy to develop and follow a wealth plan, the challenge lies not in starting the race but enduring until the end, even in the midst of setbacks, challenges and difficulties. Your staying power will be the difference maker in your journey, and the best way to remain focused is to regularly surround and saturate your mind and environment with your vision, mission, purpose and benefits. This will keep you inspired, focused and determined.

The biggest mistake most people make is to think the financial freedom journey is easy. It's simple but not easy. It requires hard work combined with a level of personal discipline and sacrifice that few will understand. You have the power to make your dream come true but it will require focus, hard work, determination and persistence. Financial freedom has to be earned and then maintained, and you do it one day at a time.

Interestingly, achieving financial freedom doesn't mean it will always be there – creating wealth is not the same as protecting wealth. New knowledge, skills and wisdom will be required to protect what you have created. Once you have created wealth you would have the character, skills and habits to re-create wealth should you lose it for whatever reason. This was one of your reasons for seeking financial freedom – to be the kind of person who deserves to achieve their goal.

It's important that you choose your vehicle for your journey and tailor your plan and strategy to suit your personal preferences. If you believe you can achieve financial freedom by playing offensive or defensive, that's great. However, I recommend both.

I don't believe in living beyond your means like I don't think living within your means and never experiencing life is the right solution. I believe you should have life and have it abundantly which means living well. Therefore, it's important to tailor your lifestyle choices to suit your preferences. Although it's exciting to create, save and invest money, it doesn't necessarily capture the true essence of living well so take the time to design a fun-filled lifestyle for yourself.

I had to make sacrifices along my journey. On several occasions I have sacrificed beyond what most would consider to be comfortable. I was willing to endure the inconvenience and delay gratification to make my dreams reality. And today I can wake up without the chains around my heart, soul and mind because I am free. The rewards greatly exceeds the sacrifices I had to make.

You too can chart a similar course, but remember that true freedom is your right and power to decide, every time, how anything or anybody can or will affect you.

I wish you freedom.

AFTERWORD

My sincere gratitude goes out to you for investing your time and life in this book and allowing me to share my thoughts and life experiences with you.

You now have a step by step pathway to wealth, financial freedom and prosperity. I am convinced that the strategies and suggestions will help you achieve your financial goals and dreams. But reading is not enough. I ask that you go away and diligently apply each technique in this book until they are transformed beyond habits to a lifestyle. Repetition is the architect of all accomplishment so I encourage you to read and re-read this book each month until you begin to see the desired changes in your thoughts, habits, lifestyle and finances. When you read this book for the second or the third time, you will discover something new but more importantly you also see something in yourself that you never knew existed before.

It is my hope that the contents of this book help you build a financial fortress around you and your loved ones so nothing can get through.

We may never meet in person, but through this book I believe we have. I would like to hear from you, so please write to me at Mensah@MensahOteh.com or contact me through my website at www.MensahOteh.com or any of my other social media channels. I would like to get to know you.

Mensah Oteh

① 2020 PJVC

Fish Time — A0 to 2PM
Scales Open/close @ 3PM (sharp)
Cook/EAT 3:30 - 4:30
Awards 4:30 / Raffle?
Lights out 5:00

~~~~~~~~~~~~~~~~~~~~~~

Menu   Cook U Own Steak (NY Strip)
                                    6-8 oz — club
        Tossed Salad   cook
        Baked Potot.   ———— club cook
OR   Roasted Chicken (Yeers) — club cook
other   Cookie Tray   — Buy
        BYOB / Soda / Iced Tea etc

~~ Save-the-Date   Taste Rite Meats
                            cost 1 person
                            steak / Potato / Salad?
                            50-60 people